A TIME AND PLACE FOR MIRTH AND MISCHIEF

By John Corbett

Published 1998

A Time and Place For Mirth and Mischief

Published by
Lough Ree Publishing Company
McCarrick Business Centre
Dublin Road
Athlone
Tel:– (0902) 74194

Front Cover design by: Francis Kennedy, Athenry.
Printed by Temple Printing Co. Ltd., Athlone.

CONTENTS

Introduction

Appendices

ACKNOWLEDGEMENTS

I would like to thank the Galway Rural Development Organisation for grant-aiding this project.

Mr. Brendan Geraghty and his team were courteous and helpful at all times.

Mr. Francis Kennedy, (Athenry), created the cartoons and the cover-piece.

The following people provided photographs, documents, medals and other material:
Michael Blehein N.T.(Gurteen),Bernie and Frank Burke(Colemanstown), The Carr Family(Gurteen), Joe Cogavin(Gurteen),Seamus Cogavin (Ballyglass), The Coppinger Family, Killuane (Marie Deely) (New Inn), Kevin Devally(Athenry),Mollie and Mary Dilleen(Gurteen P. O.),Alfie and Josephine Doyle(Colemanstown),Martin Finnerty(Clonkeenkerrill),MattieFinnerty(Glenard Crescent,Galway),Sean Ford (Circular Road,Galway), Sean Ford (Taylors Hill,Galway) , Mrs. K. Hogan(Cloncagh),Tommy Hynes (Keave),Mrs. Kelleher (Barrack St.,Lougbrea), Jimmy and Nora Kelly(Cappalusk),Ann and John Kelly(Corsgeagh),John Kenny (Cappalusk), Johnnie Kenny (Hampstead), Tom and Des Kenny (Kenny's Bookshop, Galway), Sharon Laheen(Menlough),The Late Triona Lally(Killuane),Margie McGann(Attymon), Bernie Mannion(Killuane),John Mannion (Cappalusk),Paddy Mannion(Fairhill, Menlough), Brid and Eamon Mitchell(Ace of Hearts, Gurteen),Michael Mitchell N.T.(Menlough), Aiden Molloy(Attymon), Tom 0' Neill(Glentane),Mrs. Mai Roche(Glentane), The Ruane Family(Mount Hazel), Ollie Ruane(Corsgeagh), Padraigh Ruane(Colemanstown),Martin

Scarry (Attyregan), Paddy Tierney(Alloon).Mrs. White(Kilconnell), and the White Family(Ballymacward).

Thanks to Tom O'Grady and Gurteen Community Council; Michael Kilgannon,N.T.,Ballymacward Community Council; Pat and Mary Burke,Martina Hardiman and all the members of St.Kerrill's Festival Committee.

I would like to express my appreciation for the help I received from:

The Galway Archaeological and Historical Society; who gave permission to publish extracts from their journals, Pat McMahon, Co. Librarian; The Clare Champion, Ennis, and finally The Staff of N.U.I. Library, Galway,especially Margaret Hughes, Menlough.

Introduction

The purpose of this anthology is to introduce readers to colourful characters and events of earlier times. Although the stories deal with variety of characters from the Ballymacward Gurteen region, many episodes are full of fun and will appeal to all who appreciate folklore and entertainment. The book aims to deepen the public's awareness of the beauty and treasures of rural Ireland which often pass unnoticed.

THE SCENE OF THE ACTION

Ballymacward~Gurteen is in North-East Galway more than a dozen miles from the town of Ballinasloe. It is the largest parish in the diocese of Clonfert and has a population in excess of one thousand people. Forests, hills, pasture land and bogs are to be found here and up to recent times the inhabitants supported themselves by farming. However, farming has become a part-time occupation and most people nowadays find employment in towns and cities. Small by urban standards, the area has a thriving business community. There are four licenced premises,some of which combine to make up its seven grocery shops. There are two agricultural and hardware stores and three mechanical repair centres dealing with cars, tractors and farm machinery. We have two Catholic churches, two primary schools and a total of five cemeteries. Part of St. Cuan's College is also located within the perimeters of the parish.

The waterworks and reservoir are in Mounthazel. These combine with Caltra reservoir to provide water for Bailymacward and its environs. Our sports complexes are at Alloon,

Cappalusk and Colemanstown. Hurling, Gaelic football, Camogie and Soccer are catered for at these venues and teams using them have been very successful. For example, Colemanstown Soccer Club has competed with and beaten some of the best teams in the county. Pearse's Hurling and Camogie teams have both captured All-Ireland titles. The Social Centre, which replaced the two parochial halls has been put to good use too. Dances, discos, plays and concerts have been held there and local groups have availed of it to prepare for various talent competitions.

Pearse's Ballad Group, who have won so many singing contests, rehearse there regularly. Parishioners using the centre have done equally well with Macra na Feirme, Pioneers, Scor-na-n-Og, Tops of the Clubs and other organisations. In recent years, dances have been confined to lounges and youngsters often travel to outside areas like Ballyfa, Monivea and Mountbellew to attend discos.

Natural amenities

Loughnahinch is the largest lake around, enclosing 30 acres of water. It is situated near Menlough and contains a wooded islet once used as an open-air dancing centre. Other lakes are at Shanballymore and Loch Teigue, both at the western side of the parish, close to Tiaquin. The lakes have plenty of coarse fish such as pike perch and roach. The water line dividing east from west also runs through the parish, with some local rivers flowing eastward to Ballinasloe and the remainder joining the Corrib in Galway. The rivers used to have an abundance of fish but stocks have fallen drastically owing to pollution and drainage. For this reason anglers depend mainly on the lakes for their catches.

The highest ground in Connacht is to be found here and some areas are almost four hundred feet over sea level. Croagh Patrick, the Connemara Hills and part of counties Clare and Roscommon can be viewed on clear days. Indeed some locals claim that when visibility is exceptionally good that the Wicklow Hills can be seen from Killuane Churchyard. Sceptics dispute this but if the claim is true then the east and west coasts of Ireland are viewable from within the parish boundaries.

RELICS OF 'OLD DECENCY'

In the Post Famine era the Society of Friends, better known as The Quakers, set up a model farm in Colemanstown. This had numerous buildings, each of which catered for a particular agricultural activity. The Quakers hoped that Colemanstown style farms would encourage the peasantry of the time to become more proficient in land husbandry thereby growing more food for themselves and lessening the likelihood of food scarcity in the future. When the Quakers left, the property was purchased by James Smith from Cavan. The Land Commission later took over the holding and divided it among local residents. Colemanstown House like other mansions in the area was demolished, but most of the trees in the wooded avenue leading to it are still standing. A local man, Alfie Doyle, has produced a marvellous replica of the Colemanstown farmyard. Other big houses were at Hampstead, Whitepark, Mount Bernard and Mount Hazel. The Stackpooles lived at Mount Hazel. One could visit the beautiful "pleasure grounds" there with its expansive array of shrubs, flowers, fruits and trees up to the late forties. Although the mansions attached to these estates have been demolished, visitors can still glean traces of their beauty and grandeur by observing the ruins at Mt. Bernard and Hampstead. There were forges at Kinreask and Cappalusk. Watermills for grain grinding were at Rafterys of Attyregan and Mannions of Mount Hazel. The latter was still in operation in the 1950's. Plans to restore it and upgrade Lougnahinch are being mooted at the moment.

We have two primary Schools. Excellent teachers have contributed enormously to the academic success of pupils attending them. Parents play a positive role in fundraising and over the years they have combined with the teaching staff to empower pupils to engage in a wide range of extra curricular activities. These include - hurling, camogie, football, soccer, community games and a host of talent competitions.

HISTORY AND PREHISTORY

It is believed that the parish was inhabited as far back as two thousand B.C. Evidence to support this theory is the prehistoric burial site at Annagh which was accidentally revealed by council workers attempting to widen the road there in the 1970's. Other places of interest are the ringed forts at Creeraun, one of the ancestral homes of the famous O'Kelly clan. One of the earliest churches, traces of which can still be seen is in Mounthazel near the border with Coolock bog. Then, there is the mysterious Crossmaloo located at Mannion's field and finally there are the ruins of two churches at Killuane and Clonkeenkerrill. The latter contains the body of St. Kerrill and other church dignitaries. There is an underground passage leading from the Abbey which has never been fully explored.

A CALL TO ARMS

John Houghegan, Ballyglass and John Jones, Hampstead were hanged and a number of others were imprisoned for their involvement in the United Irish Rebellion of 1798. The executions took place in Galway city. on 18th March 1799.

In common with most parts of Ireland, social and political agitation continued to develop right throughout the 1800's. The authorities hoped to quell this by introducing and reform but their policies failed miserably and the activities of The Whiteboys 8 Ribbonmen continued unabated.   Drilling in this area took place in Scarry's field prior to Pearse's insurrection and units of the I.R.A. were formed and these engaged in numerous   seditious   campaigns.   Tom   Flanagan, (Liscune,Martin Tierney, Alloon, were the principal leaders in the Ballymacward area;   while Hubert Molloy, Attymon,and Tim Scarry, Cappalusk (who later moved to Attyregan), led the Gurteen Battalion. This group was responsible for the burning of Gurteen R.I.C. barracks.   It was unoccupied at the time because the unit had tricked the constables into believing that the life and property of a Colemanstown landlord was under attack. When the R.I.C. men returned to base they were forced to leave the village and search for alternative accommodation. The I.R.A. also helped to promote Gaelic games.The British Government strenuously opposed these and banned all sporting events which promoted Irish culture. A hurling match in defiance of the ban was held in Cappalusk. The District Inspector from Athenry arrived with a contingent of R.I.C. men to stop the illegal game.   They failed to do so. When hurling sliotars were captured by the policemen in one field, players moved to other locations,acquired new sliotars and continued on with their game. The attempt to sabotage the game end ed in fiasco. To make matters worse for the inspector, while he and his forces were trying to stop the hurling match, a group of Republicans slipped into the grounds of the barracks and removed the harness that he needed to take him back to Athenry. One can only imagine the "dressing down" given to the officer left in charge of the barracks. Other areas followed the lead given by Gurteen and eventually the ban on Gaelic Games was dropped by the British Government. A number of men were arrested and charged in connection with the hurling incident but the case against them was dropped because of the confusion concerning the exact location of the match. After "Bloody Sunday," when the infamous Black And Tans killed a number of spectators and players in Croke Park, Tom Cogavin from Gurteen and his colleagues on the Galway team played in a match there to show that the spirit of the Irish people remained undaunted in spite of the massacre.

FAMOUS PEOPLE

We are proud of those parishioners who distinguished themselves in so many fields throughout the ages. Local people have made valuable contributions to politics, literature and technology and the following is a list of the better known ones.
Sean MacGillarnath, (Sean Ford) of Killuane, a friend of Padraig Pearse was a prolific writer and edited the revolutionary paper, An Claideamh Solais for a time. This distinguished scholar was popular in legal and academic circles and his visits to the locality were eagerly looked forward to by all in sundry. A Sinn Féin judge prior to independence, he was appointed District Justice in the Galway area when the Irish Government assumed power.
Professor Michael Tierney, Alloon was Chancellor of

University College Dublin. He married Evelyn MacNeill and was a member of the first Cumann na nGael government, having been returned for one of the Mayo constituencies.

In 1982, Gurteen got its first TD when Noel Treacy of Clough was elected for the Fianna Fáil party in East Galway. He is currently Minister of State in the Department of Education, Science and Technology.

The ancestors of former president of Ireland, Sean T. O'Kelly hailed from Creeraun, near the ring forts and the newly erected Telecom Eireann mast.

Among the parish's writers is John Flynn, who produced a comprehensive history of Ballymacward. John is the son of the late Dennis Flynn whose exploits are dealt with in another chapter.

John Scarry of Capalusk was a regular contributor to one of Ireland's natiional dailies up to the time of his death.

Ronnie Bellew from Banogues presently writes for national and provincial newspapers.

Martin Finnerty, Tample, was another literary figure who wrote many historical articles, some of which featured in the Galway Observer.

Richard Scarry, the famous author of children's books, visited here a number of times and has relatives in Attyregan.

Killuane's Tommy Roche is probably the best known parishioner at the moment. He was our first lotto millionaire and over the years has been responsible for a string of inventions. These include a pole erector, bale wrapper and turf turner. He founded the Roco manufacturing company which is based in Claregalway.

Killuane's Tommy Roche is probably the best known parishioner at the moment. He was the first lotto millionaire in the parish and over the years he has been responsible for a string of inventions. These include a pole erector, bale wrapper and turf turner, to mention just a few.

LABOUR AND LEISURE

Prior to the sixties most work was done by hand or by using horse drawn equipment. Ploughs, harrows, mowing machines, slanes, wheelbarrows slides and "tumbling paddies" were common in those days. The last two were contraptions for gathering hay and in the case of the slide one had to be careful when operating it as it had long sharp prongs attached to it. A certain amount of skill was needed to utilise these items but the most essential ingredient was lashings of "elbow grease".

Threshing, horse shoeing, haymaking, turfcutting and grain harvesting were social as well as working occasions because they gave people opportunities to come together and to get to know one another better. Market and fair days were particularly useful. On these days poultry, animals and agricultural produce changed hands while rustics chatted, drank or argued over prices. Selling stock often became a communal affair as friends, neighbours and tanglers all contributed to the making of the deal.

Bringing stock to a fair was no easy task. One had to be on the road early to get the best results. Mountbellew and Athenry were the nearest cattle selling places although Castleblakeney and Kilconnell used to host fairs in earlier times. When cattle and sheep had been disposed of, buyers and sellers would retire to licensed saloons for refreshment. Then the herdowners and their helpers would set out for home on foot or by bicycle.

In those times of limited incomes, rabbit trapping was a profitable source of income for a minority of parishioners. One trapper claimed that he could make more money at this business in a few months than he could earn for the rest of the year from other employments.

In the line of pastimes,' pitch and toss 'was very popular with young men. Of course there were running, jumping and tug o'war contests also. Hurling and football were played too but organised matches were rare in the early part of the century and rules were less clearly defined than at present. Handball was extremely popular. There are handball alleys at either end of the parish and at one time players had to form queues in order to play matches in them. Visiting teams came here to play and handballers from Ballymacward-Gurteen had several successes at competitions throughout the country. There was plenty of free entertainment and participation was open to everyone. This changed with the advent of ballrooms and marquees.

In the Summer, crossroad dances and "maypoles" were well attended and these were later replaced by marquees and discos. Card playing usually came into its own during the winter months. Storytelling too reached a wide audience. People like Pat Murray and Walter McDonagh of Esker, Johnnie Mitchell of Garafine, Pat Kenny of Cappalusk and Martin Larkin and Paddy Kilkenny of Kinreask used to regale their listeners with their repertoire of folk tales and legends.

In the country house dances, talented performers like Tom Power, Johnnie Kelly, the Callinans, Corbetts, Finnertys, Kilkennys, Lydons, Hessions, Jimmie Dwyer, J Laffey, Jimmy

Dullaghan, "Inky" Craven and the Duffys provided music and aural entertainment for generations of revellers.

Plays and concerts were usually well attended. Seamus Duffy, Paddy Kelly, Packie Mentane, Mick Neary and Tom Cormican invariably gave excellent performances. Nerves or stage fright were unknown to them and when in difficulty, they often improvised with pieces of their own which equalled or excelled the work of the original author.

Horse, pony and greyhound races were held in Gurteen and Ballymacward at different times and again these were highly successful.

In the past both labour and leisure required effort and commitment. However, there were lots of opportunities for self expression and enjoyment and happily the majority of the inhabitants fully availed of these.

Law and Disorder

Above-This grocery and licensed premises once housed the R.I.C. barracks in Gurteen.

This lounge was formerly an R.I.C. station in Ballymacward. It was closed in the 1890's and constables there transferred to Castleblakeney and Woodlawn. Menlough and Kilconnell stations took over the job of policing the area at a later date. But in Gurteen the barracks was taken over by the Irish Government and was used by gardai for several decades. Except once when there were protests about the sale of land in Creeraun, illegal activity in this period was negligible. It must have been quite an ordeal for officers to confine their attention to legal matters since the majority of court cases concerned unlicensed dogs and unlit bicycles. One liquor loving law man, Clare born, John Hastings, regarded bread soda as the best cure for his ailing stomach after a bout of alcohol. He used to send Leitrim man, Garda John McHugh to Menlough for some, whenever
supplies of bread soda ran out in Gurteen. McHugh sometimes took longer than expected on the errand and Hastings was often heard to declare that, "A man would be dead and damned before that bloody fool would bring relief". Although not quite as peaceful as it was in the early part of the century, nevertheless the crime rate is low and one can enjoy the delights of the district without fear of being molested in any way

CHAPTER ONE

PASTORS, PREACHERS AND PLAYBOYS

In the early part of the century there were numerous parishioners ready willing and able to test their strength against all
comers. Among them were Brian Mannion, Pat Kenny, Joe
Ford Tom Kenny and Mickey Bums.

Tom Kenny once pulled a cart containing a ton of meal across
a fifty metre stretch of yard.
This was an achievement in itself but what made it more
remarkable was the fact that his three "helpers" were doing
their utmost to pull against rather than with him.

Mickey Burns was reputed to have knocked out a British
army boxer at one stage and this coupled with rows involving
the R.I.C. established his reputation as a person not to be
lightly provoked. Mickey had a goat that used to play
havoc with neighbours' crops. He was footing turf one day
when a lady came to complain about the goat. She began a
litany of abuse but Mickey kept on working and didn't raise his
head. Eventually she got so angry that the noise she was making frightened Mickeys' dog who began to bark. Mickey turned
to the dog and said, "Shut up. You should know better anyway".
The confrontation ended in victory for Mickey. The lady left
without further comment and Mickey and his canine friend
were left in peace for the rest of the day.

1

MISTAKEN IDENTITY

The goat attracted attention of another kind later. A young schoolboy named Mickey Cooke saw the animal for the first time when working in a field with his mother. He was amazed at the sight of this strange creature. He asked his mother what it was and she told him it was The Devil. He caused quite a sensation at school next day when he announced what he had seen. He was taken to the various classrooms while pupils and teachers listened attentively to his description of the goat, with its horns, beard and the chains which rattled loudly as it moved. This continued for some time .At last the boy realised that the whole affair was being treated as a joke. After having repeated the story several times, the teacher said, "Now will you tell us again what The Devil looked like?" The boy answered, "Just like you, Mam." No further questions were asked about "the apparition" which the Cookes had seen.

A SHORT SHRIFT

The final piece about Mickey refers to the time he went to confession to a missioner. The latter was very severe on the question of temperance and when Burns confessed to having been on a drinking binge, the missioner refused to give him absolution. Mickey left the confessional box and went to
another confessor in the same church. On being asked how long it was since his last confession he replied, "About two minutes ago, Father."

A SWORDSMAN FROM THE CITY

But of course countryfolk weren't responsible for all the amusing antics that took place in their midst. Townsfolk and city dwellers contributed to the mirth also. One such person was Charlie Butterly, who was born in Swords in Co. Dublin but who married and spent most of his life in the west of Ireland.

He was a tradesman, noted for his witty comments, especially in matters relating to food. Questioned about the dinner menu at one of his work places, he said, "Cabbage and potatoes" in a loud voice. Then he added the word "meat" in a very low tone, indicating to his listeners that this was in short supply.

"It looks like rain," said one hostess. She was looking out the window while she filled his cup. "It does surely," said Charlie, "But it smells like tea." Later she asked, "How would you like your egg cooked ,Charlie?"

"With another," was the reply.

A Skehana curate hired him to plaster a wall. Progress was slow and the priest said, "I could do that myself only for the latting." Charlie replied, "Sure I could read Mass too only for the Latin."(This was in the pre Vatican Two era before church services came to be celebrated in the vernacular.) The last of the anecdotes concerning the Liffeysider had to do with a landlord who was very stingy with his workmen. Meat was seldom served and the labourers often left the table with appetites that hadn't been fully satisfied. Then an old boar died. The meat was cooked and given to the diners. As can be imagined, it was tough and unsavoury and the workers were not impressed with it. Grace before meals was always said and on the second day it was Charlie's turn to recite it. This was his prayer:

> Oh God on high who rules the sky,
> Look down upon us four.
> Give us meat that we can eat
> And take away this boar!

MEN OF THE CLOTH

Many notable clerics have been associated with the parish. Fr. Michael Griffin of Gurteen was ordained in 1917.

He was an active supporter of the Republican cause and was murdered in 1920, presumably by agents of the British government. His body was found buried in a shallow grave in Barna bog. It was reinterred later in the grounds of St. Brendan's Cathedral in Loughrea. Fr. Tom Naughton was another kind of rebel. He was reprimanded by the P.P. Fr. Joseph Pelly for insulting one of the Stackpoole family. The incident occurred when the P.P. and curate were invited to a Christmas meal at Mounthazel. In the course of the conversation the Duke de Stackpoole's son claimed to be fluent in French and Spanish but failed to live up to expectations when challenged by Fr. Naughton. The latter had studied abroad and was fluent in both languages. The Stackpooles were embarrassed by their son's failure to display his linguistic skill and Fr. Pelly was so annoyed by the incident that he made excuses and both priests left almost immediately. Fr. Pelly vented his anger on his companion and said he would see to it that his stay in the parish would be a short one. Unmoved, Fr. Naughton replied that he was willing to leave whenever the Bishop so desired.

Fr. Pelly's threat never materialised because Fr. Naughton was appointed P.P. in 1936. He was a popular pastor who liked his drink. He had some narrow escapes when his car went out of control and he found himself upturned in fields and bushes once or twice. He also raised the hackles of traditionalists when he questioned the authenticity of St. Kerrill at a religious ceremony in Gurteen.

DIGGER "DRAGS HIS FEET" OVER DEAD DONKEY

While he was in Ballymacward a donkey died in the vicinity of the parochial house. He selected Mick Neary to dispose of the dead animal. The burial fee of ten shillings was paid in advance. However when the money had been paid, Mick made himself scarce and eventually the stench from the donkey forced the priest to seek another "undertaker". When Neary heard the donkey had been dispatched, he arrived at the presbytery and proceeded to search the grounds for the carcass, Fr.Naughton observed this charade through a window. When Mick abandoned the search and headed for Kynes, the priest followed him He hoped to embarrass Neary by demanding his money back. Hot words occurred between the pair and the clergyman ordered Kyne not to serve the unreliable undertaker.

At this point Mick went to fill the drink himself. Neary was threatened with dire consequences, supernatural and otherwise if he persisted in serving himself. He refused to yield, and Fr. Naughton burst out laughing and the stand-to came to an end as Fr. Naughton declared that he "was the biggest scoundrel in Ireland". Fr. O'Neill of Ballinastack a World War one veteran was a fondly regarded figure beloved by his people. He was noted for his generosity and for his healing powers. Several people claimed miraculous recoveries due to his intervention. His last appointment was at Cappatagle and his fondness for giving general absolution did nothing to lessen his popularity. At the other end of the spectrum was Fr. Michael O'Reilly, curate in Gurteen from 1936 - 1947. He was a strong man with strong views on sexual, social and political matters. He expected his congregation to be seated well in advance of Mass time. Chapel doors were locked before the service began, therefore those who came late were locked out while the early birds were imprisoned within the church. Martin Finnerty of Tample arrived one Sunday just after the doors had been locked. When h saw what had happened, he blessed himself, genuflected and set off for home remarking, "Virtue is its own reward". Late Mass goers in Fr. O'Reilly's time used to assemble in a shed adjacent to the church, where according to reports, cardplaying and gossip featured more prominently than prayers, psalms or hymn singing. Fr. Michael also made his presence felt at dances and attempted to enforce strict sexual segregation. Despite his best efforts, many illicit liasons were formed. The Romeos and their unfortunate partners could expect to receive a severe tongue lashing at the very least. Unmarried mothers and their offspring were obliged to leave in order to hide their disgrace. Fr. Michael was ever willing to inform "undesirables" of his opinion of them and such was the power of the clergy at the time that the majority of them were prepared to obey his strictures.

On the other hand, he was genuinely interested in the success of his people. He encouraged those who were struggling economically and was responsible for clearing up the debt incurred in the building of St. Michaels church.

Many changes have taken place since Fr. O'Reilly's time and modern clergymen play a more passive role in social affairs than he did. In recent times they have concentrated their efforts on church renovations and the building of parochial houses.

Prominent clerics associated with the parish include the late Monsignor Callinan appointed P.P. in 1945 and Dr. John Kirby, Bishop of Clonfert who assisted Fr. Dunne between 1974 and 1977.

Then of course there is Fr. Nicholas Murray of Esker who was deeply involved in sport and was once regarded as the most promising hurler in the county. Fr. Nicholas spent a good deal of time in the Phillipines and is currently in charge of the Columban Order.

At the time this material is being compiled the parish is under the spiritual guidance of two worthy gentlemen, Fr. Vincent Lawless, C.C. of Gurteen and Fr. John Slattery, P.P. of Ballymacward.

It is not possible to mention all the priests who worked in the parish throughout the years but I think it's fair to say that they've all contributed positively to country life and have made their presence felt one way or another.

CHAPTER TWO
The curious capers of a country curate

By and large clergymen are solid individuals who follow the teachings of the Gospels faithfully. They aim to inspire their parishioners by the example and piety of their own personal lives. Occasionally, however, there comes a daredevil divine whose zest for life sets his flock an example of a different kind. Such a man was Patrick O'Loughlin, a curate in the parish of Gurteen, Co. Galway who took up duty in the year 1906. From the beginning the signs were that he would be an adventurous pastor and subsequent years proved these signs to be correct.

His early years

Fr, O'Loughlin began by devising an unusual method of fund raising. He acquired a wooden floor which was to be used for

dancing. What made this unique was the fact that the dances were to be held on an islet in the middle of a local lake! The lake itself was located in the heart of a bog and boats were used to ferry dancers to and from the island. The fee for the round trip including admission to the dances was the princely sum of six old pence (this was probably prohibitive in those days when the price of a pint was two and a half pence). The dances were highly successful and drew huge crowds from surrounding areas. A local poet wrote:

> *There was music on the islet*
> *There were boatloads by the score,*
> *Who joined the fun and revelry,*
> *On that brightly varnished floor.*

> *Father Pat O'Loughlin*
> *Provided floor and bench*
> *Half sets and old time waltzes*
> *Were danced in Loughnahinch*

Eventually, however, these outdoor island dances fell foul of the weather.
Another verse states:

> *The crowds kept ever growing,*
> *They thought 'twould last for years,*
> *But the cruel Irish climate*
> *Changed all their smiles to tears.*
> *On a fateful summer's evening*
> *Came a mighty shower to drench*
> *That group of happy dancers*
> *on the banks of Loughnahinch.*

Although Fr. O'Loughlin was not a man to give up easily, further rain continued to dampen the spirits of the patrons so inevitably the dances on the islet came to an end.

MOVING WITH THE TIMES.

As can be imagined, Fr. 0 Loughlin made many friends (and possibly a few enemies also) in the district. In those days motor cycles had just arrived on the scene and Fr. Patrick lost no time in purchasing one. This was to cause him some difficulty. He didn't have any trouble starting the machine, but stopping it was an entirely different matter. He used to run the bike against a ditch or solid object in order to bring it to a halt. Alternatively he would keep it in motion until the petrol ran out. He must have used the second method frequently because, according to reports, he was often seen careering recklessly through flocks of sheep or cattle unheedful of the anger or curses of the unfortunate stock owners.

A PAINFUL PARTING.

Fr. Patrick continued to travel on his motorbike uneventfully for some time. Then one day he had brain wave. It suddenly occurred to him that this marvellous machine could be used to generate enough speed to propel not one- but two individual~ along the Irish country roads. He needed a human guinea pig to test his theory and his choice was a local teacher, named Miss Owens. She was persuaded to link her vehicle, an ordinary bicycle, by means of a rope cord to Fr. 0' Loughlin's motor cycle. The experiment went well- for the first half mile. Then as the couple began to gain in speed and confidence, the cord suddenly snapped and the hapless Miss Owens went flying head over heels into a neighbour' s yard. Fr. Patrick continued on for some time blissfully unaware that he and his partner had parted company. Eventually the truth dawned on him and he returned to find his erstwhile friend being comforted and bandaged by neighbours. At this point the pair exchanged a few 'unchristian' civilities and shortly afterwards returned to their respective homes - Miss Owens on bruised and battered limbs and Fr. Patrick on his trusty motor-bike.

REMEMBERING THE EVENT

Josie Hynes, a local poet, wrote a parody on the song-" The Girl I Left Behind Me"-to commemorate the event. Here are some of the lines;

> *Going down the fall,*
> *I heard the call,*
> *Sever the cord that binds me.*
> *And when I looked around,*
> *Flat on the ground,*
> *Was the girl I tied behind me.*

> *Neary and Roche,*
> *They did the most,*
> *They treated me most kindly.*
> *The wounds being sore,*
> *They could do no more,*
> *For the girl I tied behind me.*

The poem had the effect of imprinting Fr. O'Loughlins name indelibly in the folklore of the district. These are just some of the legends associated with this great clergyman. Excitement and adventure were the hallmarks of Fr. Patrick's reign. He was replaced in 1921 by a more conventional priest named Fr. O'Neill. There have been many curates since, but none of them has ever captured the imagination to the same extent as Fr. O'Loughlin. Only once in several lifetimes, it seems, is a parish destined to acquire such a colourful and swashbuckling clergyman.

A LIVELY PARISH

During his curacy the good priest encouraged the people to enjoy themselves. He as not averse to "treading the light fantastic" himself and he as a popular guest at all local gatherings. He also produced plays and concerts in the local hall and these no doubt helped to shorten the long winter nights for his parishioners and his achievements in this area no doubt encouraged many actors and actresses in Ballymacward-Gurteen long after Fr. Patrick's departure.

A Determined Man

Fr. Patrick was an assertive individual who usually managed to get his own way. One one occasion he insisted that a villager who had hosted house stations the previous Autumn should host them again the following Spring. (House stations consisted of having a Mass on the premises and inviting neighbours for a meal and celebration afterwards.) Normally a householder would be expected to have these once in a five to six year period, but this unfortunate villager was obliged to hold them secondly because no other house in the district was in adequate state of repair at this particular time.

His persuasive power was also evident from the speed in which he obtained funding for his dance floor in Loughnahinch. In the case of the dancing venture Fr. O'Loughlin was undeterred by the opposition of neighbouring parish priests who voiced strong opposition to it. Fr. Patrick refused to share the profits of the dances with the parish priests in Menlough, even though part of the lake was in the latter's parish. Many people felt that the demise of the open air dances was due in no small part to the intervention of the parish priest who sought divine assistance and through his superior powers was able to produce unexpected cloudbursts on the dancing patrons on at least one occasion.

Whatever about the merits of these theories, once the dances had been abandoned, no serious effort was ever made to revive them and the wooden dance floor which was used on the islet was transported to the mainland and still functions as a ceiling for one of the cottages in the neighbourhood.Several curates have come and gone since Fr. O'Loughlin's time, but none of them has ever made the same impression as this colourful cleric who brightened up the lives of his parishioners over seven decades ago.

Chapter three

TOM, THE COUNTRY PLAYBOY

Tom Cormican was a farmer who lived in Corsgeagh. He was a stout, blue-eyed man who took part in numerous plays and concerts and his forte was his portrayal of comic characters in local dramatic productions.

FOOLS AND HORSES

Tom was interested in horse-racing and owned a number of animals that featured in this sport. One such steed, Blazing Furze, was running a Ballymacward races and Tom persuaded many local patrons to back the animal. Unfortunately for him and for them, Blazing Furze was not among the winners. The local parish priest, Fr. Pelly, who had backed him heavily, confronted the owner and said, "I always thought you were a fool Cormican, but I never saw it proved until today". Tom smiled provocatively and retorted, "By the look of things, there were a few more fools besides myself here today." Another punter was so upset over his losses that he went around the racecourse muttering "Blazing shit , Blazing shit. The Devil take yourself and your Blazing Furze".

Tom took a special delight in turning serious occasions to laughter. At that time, some of the senior citizens in the parish used to congregate at a shant (shed) to discuss important farming events. Tom was present at such a meeting after the annual Fair in Ballinasloe. As one would expect, the conversation was about horses and the big deals that were made the day before. When the discussion was in full flow, Tom stood up and said, "Do ye know what I'm going to tell ye men?" As he as was known to be very interested in horses, he received maximum attention from all those present. He continued, "Paid in his Own Coin is as good a play as was ever written provided it is properly produced." This incongruous comment was greeted with exclamations of disgust. Our hero was told in no uncertain terms what they thought of him and was advised "to go home and not be makin' an eejit" of himself.

TREADING THE BOARDS

Just as Elizabethans disapproved of female thespians, some people in his era frowned on the idea of country folk "making exhibitions of themselves" on stage. Tom enjoyed annoying people of this kind. He was drawing hay one day when he saw one of these "wise" men approaching. The road was narrow and as each of them had a cart, it would be necessary for one of them to give way. Tom got a script of a play he was rehearsing and placed it in front of his face. He continued on along the road until he almost collided with the man in the oncoming cart. Then at the last minute, he pulled in to the side of the road and said with a look of feigned surprise, "Oh is that you Larry? I never saw you coming. This stage work is very demanding. You need to do an awful lot of rehearsing beforehand."
The "wise" man was so disgusted at Tom's behaviour that all he could manage was a scowl of disdain and a few inarticulate grunts.

FUN AND FEATHERS

Tom displayed a love for alcohol early in life. He was just nineteen years of age when this came to the attention of his parents.

He was taken home from a public house in a wheelbarrow and was desposited at his own doorstep in a drunken state. His mother was deeply shocked and vented her anger on the pilot of his wheelbarrow. "I wouldn't mind", she exclaimed crossly, "But Tom was a Pioneer. He hasn't ever broken his confirmation Pledge up to now". The wheelbarrow man who was partly inebriated himself, eyed her and said, "Well if it wasn't broken then it must have been very badly bent."

Tom used a side-car when he went in search of company and refreshment. Once he was accompanied by a member of a prominent family. The pair intended to visit a public house in a nearby village which was owned by relatives of Tom's companion. They met some travellers on their way and Tom had an idea. He decided to have some fun at his companion's expense so he brought a mattress from the travellers. He nicked the mattress with a pen-knife and the two of them were covered in feathers by the time they reached the bar. The bar owners were utterly shocked at the condition of their relative but they didn't recognise Tom. One of them immediately set forth to inform the family of Tom's companion that their son "was a disgraceful blackguard, travelling around the country with a tinker." Needless to say, the young man was severely reprimanded when he returned home later that night.

DEARLY "PAID IN HIS OWN COIN"

The tables were turned on Tom, so to speak on another occasion. This time he was producing and acting in a play which he hoped would be a huge success. He had gained quite a reputation in the field of drama and he intended to use the occasion to impress the family of a lady for whom he cherished romantic aspirations. Unfortunately for him, a rival took a hand in the proceedings. Knowing Tom's fondness for alcohol he plied him with drink prior to the performance, with the result that he was totally insensible by the time the curtain rose. What was meant to be a show-case of talent turned out to be an absolute fiasco. They play began and ended almost simultaneously. As the curtain opened, Tom tottered across the stage and collapsed. He ended up in a most undignified position with his two feet in the air and the rest of his body jammed in the stage fireplace. Some loud rude noises accompanied the performance and as he curtain fell, so did Tom's chances of winning his lady-love and of impressing her parents. The lady in question later married the architect of Tom's theatrical misfortunes. This unfortunate incident, however, didn't quench our hero's love of drama and he continued to be involved in plays and concerts for several years afterwards.

GETTING A FAIR DEAL

Tom had good quality cattle and liked to attend fairs and markets that were held throughout the country. He often recalled an encounter he had with a cousin at one of these fairs. The latter was selling a cow and asked Tom to buy the animal. "As a friend", he added, "I won't be too hard on you". "When I heard what he expected for the cow", said Tom, "I shuddered to think what price he would have asked for her from a rank outsider". The Cormicans opened a small grocery shop in later years. This helped to augment the family income but what was more important, it enabled Tom to keep in touch with his neighbours without having to do any travelling. One day in the shop, a customer was describing an accident that had happened to a lady in the district. She had been making a cock of hay when she lost her balance and fell to the ground, breaking her leg in the process. The customer had been helping the lady with the hay at the time of the accident. Tom said to him, "Weren't you a terrible man to let that happen!". The customer said, "What could I have done?" "You should have put up your fork when you saw her falling and that would have saved her". The customer got a hearty fit of laughing. If he had done what Tom had suggested, the lady in question would have had much more to worry about than a mere broken leg.

PUTTING THE CART BEFORE THE HORSE

The Cormicans had a cart which needed to be repaired. Tom was sent by his mother to collect the cart, She was in charge of finances and gave him 11 pounds to cover the cost of the repairs. On his way to the carpenter's Tom met a number of gamblers, much older than himself and he joined them for a game of poker. They relieved him of his money in a short time. Then he had to face home without either cart or money. "He hasn't finished it yet", he told his mother. "Oh that's alright then" she said. "You can leave the money on the dresser".

"Well now, but I haven't got it. I gave it all to him".

"And why did you do that when he hadn't finished the cart".

"Sure he told me he wanted the money to buy wood for the cart".

When the interview was over, Tom still had to solve the problem of finding money to pay the carpenter. Luckily for him, he met a neighbour who wanted to buy a bullock. Tom told him he needed money urgently and that he would sell him a bullock at a reasonable price. He insisted on one condition however. The animal would have to be left on Cormican's land until the rest of the stock was being sold. The neighbour agreed to this and paid for the bullock, This enabled Tom to pay the carpenter and collect his cart. Villagers who knew that he had gambled the repair money were puzzled when inquiries revealed that the carpenter had been paid for his work. It was much later when the neighbour took the animal on to his own land that the mystery was finally solved for them. Tom's mother never found out about the affair. The incident was a godsend for Cormican because the sale netted him 14 pounds so this meant he had three pounds extra for himself. Knowing his fondness for refreshment, it is reasonable to assume thathe didn't allow the 'windfall' to burn a hole in his pocket.

Tom always had an ample supply of cash, but even if he didn't, he wouldn't have allowed it to interfere with his social life. Fun and laughter meant much more to him than wealth. Like most happy people, he didn't worry about the future. 'What did posterity ever do for me' he once asked, Tom Cormican lived to a ripe old age and retained his boyish sense of humour and his propensity for fun and mischief right up to the end.

THE CORMICANS

Tom, wife and child, taken more than 30 years ago

Chapter four

VISITING TIME AT CORBETTS

The Corbetts:- James and his wife Lillie with their son John taken on

the grounds of U.C.G. in the 1970's

Visiting in the rambling houses was a common feature of life in the parish in the early part of the century. These were usually thatched houses where rustics assembled for storytelling, music or dancing. One such house belonged to James Corbett. James came from Clare and settled in Gurteen in the 1930s.

Born in 1892, one of a family of six parented by John and Susan (nee Touhy) Corbett, James spent his early years in Clonkerry, approximately one mile from the village of Labasheeda. The name Labasheeda translates as Silken bed, but times were troublesome and life was certainly not a bed of silk or roses for John, Susan and family. Land agitation was widespread and peasant farmers were under constant threat of eviction if they failed to pay rent promptly or if they incurred the wrath of the landlords. The villains of the piece in this case were the Van de Leur family who owned most of the land in the district. On one occasion, bailiffs and agents were on their way to carry out evictions in the area but were prevented from doing so by their property.

T. J. Ryan, a Well Known Republican in West Clare

For some unexplained reason, the evictions did not take place subsequently and John and Susan remained in possession of their meagre holding. Considering this background, it is not surprising that James became involved in anti government activities at an early age. He was a member of the IRA and participated in a number of ambushes against Crown forces in West Clare. News of this soon reached the authorties. He was arrested and lodged in Belfast Jail. Here he and his comrades went on hunger strike to protest against their incarceration and were released, having spent twenty one days without food.

The timing of their release coincided with the quitting time of the Belfast dockyard workers and these availed of the opportunity to register their disapproval of the rebels by throwing coal at them. James was not intimidated by his internment and returned to his paramilitary activities immediately after his release.

On one occasion the infamous Black and Tans visited the Clonkerry homestead with the intention of burning the family out. They were accompanied by a Labasheeda based RIC man by the name of Foley who managed to persuade them not to go ahead with their plans. He claimed that James's father was a peaceful citizen who thoroughly disapproved of his son's behaviour. Thus the family home escaped destruction a second time.

James was elected as a Sinn Fein councillor who represented the Kildysart area. Later on he was given the task of trying to maintain some kind of law and order during those troubled times.

He was a great admirer of Michael Collins and supported the pro-treaty group during the civil war. He was stationed in Kildysart barrack and helped to defend it successfully when it was attacked by anti-treaty forces. He remained in the army during the Civil War and was demobbed when it ended in 1924. Himself and his companions were offered jobs in the civil service but rejected them on the advice of their newly formed Comrades Association who felt that the pay being offered was totally inadequate.

When he retired from the army, he spent some time farming. He married Lillie Stephens from Cranny, whose family had taken the Republican side during the Civil War. Lillie and her sister were both members of Cumann na mBan and themselves and their brothers were also involved in many daring exploits in the War of Independence.

James retired from the army with the rank of Captain but was later given the title of Commandant. After leaving Clare, he quickly adapted to his new home, he enjoyed telling his neighbours about customs from his native county One such custom involved 'Strawboys'.These were uninvited guests who used to appear at weddings dressed up in outfits made of straw, ribbons and other colourful material which covered their bodies and faces.   They would entertain the guests with music and dancing. Their display was intended as a gesture of goodwill towards the newly-weds and if they didn't make their appearance at some stage during the celebrations,then the in-laws would begin to worry about the reputation or the popularity of the spouse who was hosting the party.Likewise, parishioners discussed Galway customs that were new to James. He was particularly interested in one custom relating to wakes.This was the 'mock' wedding which was sometimes performed in the houses of deceased persons. A 'phoney' celebrant would call out the names of male and female individuals and would proceed with the marriage ceremony ,often against the wishes of the couple in question. This custom was so prevalent in some parts of Connacht that the Bishop of Elphin forbade females to attend wakes in his diocese at one time.

Music,however was the predominant feature of life at Corbetts..

Both himself and his wife played fiddle and concertina but the concertina was his favourite instrument and was popular with locals also. It was something of a novelty because prior to his arrival, the melodeon would have been the main musical instrument in the locality. Sessions at Corbetts varied in length and most tastes were catered for. Songs varied from the classical "I dream I dwelt in marble halls" to the latest American film hits of the time like "Meet me in St. Louis". Patriotic ballads such as "Boolavogue" "God Save Ireland"and 'Skibereen' featured regularly at these music sessions.Tin whistles, flutes, fiddles and of course the concertina were the main instruments. The seasons made little difference to the people who gathered there because the sound of music and dancing could be heard at all times of the year. His wife her sister Emily Stephens were responsible for refreshments and guests always received ample supplies of food and drink after their strenuouss activities & exertions on the dance floor.

James's favourite song was the ballad of Ayrlroe. Wherever there was a get together he sang this and accompanied himself on the concertina.He was one of the first people to purchase a radio. Jamesie Connor was passing the house, one evening and heard music coming from the radio. He didn't understand how radio functioned. Shortly afterwards he met a neighbour and remarked, "Corbett isn't a bad warrant to play that new contraption".

The radio of course was another attraction for visitors as very few people had one at the time. On Sunday afternoons large numbers would assemble to hear Michael O'Hehir's match commentaries.Election results and political events were closely monitored and it was interesting to observe the reaction of the listeners as they responded to the items being broadcast.

James took religion very seriously. He had great respect for the Redemtorists and other enclosed orders. He always maintained that air travel was dangerous yet he was ready to make his first flight at the age of eighty-five. This was to visit the Shrine of the Blessed Virgin Mary at Lourdes. The following year saw him boarding another plane, this time to Portugal and while there, he and his family visited Fatima. He was deeply impressed by the devotion of the pilgrims at Fatima.

Reading and walking were two pastimes he enjoyed and he engaged in both of these up to a short time before his death. He was in good health and the only time he spent in hospital was when he was released from prison. In medical matters he favoured traditional remedies and he was a great advocate of

bonesetters. He had occasion to use the services of these once or twice during his lifetime. There is a story about a famous bonesetter from Clare named Burke who was also a T.D.
He was an independent but always supported the Fianna Fail nominee in the election for Taoiseach. A Fine Gael supporter in Galway asked James to explain why Burke was so popular in Clare. James told him that he was a successful bonesetter and his services were called upon by people from all
parts of the county. The Fine Gael supporter then asked him could it be possible that there are enough broken bones in Clare to elect a man to the Dail.

Another story which James used to tell also concerned politics. In the run-up to the nineteen thirty two general election, election fever was high and John Connors from the village attended a Fianna Fail rally in Ballinasloe.He returned home that evening and visited the Fords, who were staunch Fine Gael supporters They were reciting the Rosary at the time but John was so excited about the day's events that he didn't realise they were praying . He came in and struck the table a blow with his fist and said, "You should have been there today Joeen.Dev would have opened your eyes for you". Joe looked up from his rosary beads and said, "Shut up you fool" . Mrs. Ford scolded Joe and said, "You shouldn't call John Connors a fool, Joe".Joe then said ,"And what else might I call him?".

In political matters James had a rich store of knowledge. He talked extensively about Article 12 of the Treaty and the shortcomings of the Anglo-Irish boundary Commission under the chairmanship of Judge Feetham of South Africa. He was also aware of the intense rivalry between Cathal Brugha and Michael Collins, which he claimed, was in existence long before the Treaty divisions took place.

Folklore and local legends were explored in depth and he had many interesting stories to tell his listeners. Villagers were fascinated to hear first-hand accounts of the famous Biddy Early and he was able to tell them about dealings which his own relations had with the Wise Woman of Feakle herself. James, like all rambling house hosts, took great delight in meeting friends and recalling past experiences. In those times invitations were unheard of and a warm welcome was extended to all comers. Nearly all the thatched cottages have been replaced by modern mansions but it is doubtful if the occupants will ever experience the same level of exhilaration and enjoyment which the old buildings provided. Visiting rambling houses is a thing of the past. Storytelling has been the main loser. Singing and dancing are as popular as ever, although they are now practised in modern surroundings and artists can avail of the latest technology in order to enhance their performances, unlike their predecessors in the humble whitewashed cottages of former times.

CHAPTER FIVE

FUN AND FROLICS WITH DENNIS FLYNN

Dennis Flynn was a tall fun-loving person who lived beside the

church in Ballymacward. He availed of every opportunity to enjoy himself and provided endless amusement for his neighbors. He used to travel with his son occasionally in a side car which was attached to a motor cycle. A curious neighbour wanted to know why they had bought such a "contraption". Dennis told him, "We thought 'twould be handy for going to Mass". This in spite of the fact that he lived less than twenty yards away from the church.

GETTING TO BE A BIG NOISE

Dennis was born in Galway city and moved to the country when he inherited a holding of land from his aunt. He loved travelling and a local butcher who had 'high notions'; asked him to play the role of travelling companion on a trip to Dublin. It didn't turn out to be such a good idea because Dennis decided to have himself some fun at the butcher's expense. Dennis arrived at the railway station in a tattered coat tied with a piece of string. He also wore a pair of heavy clogs. The butcher was dismayed at Dennis's appearance and would probably have cancelled the outing but for the fact that the tickets had been paid for already. Worse was to come. When they arrived in the city they received a great deal of unwelcome attention due to Dennis's slovenly attire and because of the loud clattering sound made by his clogs. (It should be remembered that in those days, city traffic was light so therefore the sound of Dennis's clogs would be much more noticeable than it would be nowadays.)

KEEPING TROUBLE AT ARM'S LENGTH

Dennis caused more commotion when the pair attempted to board a tram. He was smoking a small stump of a clay pipe and when the conductor saw it, he called out, "Smokers up on top please".

Dennis pretended not to understand him and responded with a loud, "HAW?". The conductor repeated the message and then Dennis remarked, "Oh, you mane the loft? He wants us up in the loft La'".

When they finally boarded the vehicle the butcher seated himself as far away from Dennis as possible. Unfortunately, this did not improve matters at all. Dennis placed himself among some well-dressed commuters and continued to embarrass his companion by calling his attention to all the wonderful "tingeens" (things) that were to be seen from the top of the tram.

The situation continued like this for most of the day. In the afternoon, the travellers went to a restaurant to have a meal. At the beginning of the meal, Dennis was mute enough and the butcher had reason to feel hopeful at last. Taking advantage of the lull, he struck up conversation with a smartly dressed lady who happened to be manageress of the restaurant. She responded warmly to the butcher's company and the conversation was in full flow when Dennis interrupted again. He inserted his fingers in a chocolate cake that had been placed on a tray on the table and held it up in front of the astonished face of the manageress.

"How much is this?" he asked.

"Five shillings", she replied.

"And half that?" Dennis asked.

"Two and sixpence".

"And half that again?" Dennis wanted to know.

"One and threepence".

'Oh begob I think we'll chuck in La. Shure a chunk of this 'd
be very handy
goin' home on the train".

This brought the butcher's conversation with the manageress
to an abrupt end and the two western wanderers returned home
in silence. Dennis had thoroughly enjoyed himself, but the day
had been an unmitigated disaster for the butcher who had fund-
ed the entire expedition and who had suffered humiliation and
embarrassment in return for his outlay.

KEEPING THE SPIRIT OF FUN AWAKE

Dennis liked to play to 'the gallery'. Once in his seventies, he
climbed over the chapel wall, saying to onlookers, "I thought it
a bit long to go 'round by the gate to-day." Unfortunately for
him, Fr.O'Reilly was talking to his parishioners at the time. He
disapproved of buffoonery, especially from a person as old as
Dennis. He registered his disapproval by applying his boot to
the rear portion of Dennis's anatomy, much to the amusement of
the onlookers.

Like many entertainers, Dennis could convert solemn events to occasions of mirth in a very short time. This happened at a wake in Ballymacward which he attended sometime at turn of the century - (At wakes friends assembled to mourn the passing of a loved one. Food and drink were given to the mourners by relatives of the deceased.) When the meal was being served, Dennis seated himself beside Mike Burns, a man who was easily amused. He waited until Mike had taken a large mouthful and then he made one of his funny faces at him. Mike couldn't contain himself. He sprayed a large quantity food and drink across the table, hitting one of the chief mourners and staining his new suit of clothes. Then he was overcome by uncontrollable fits of laughter. At this point, he was asked to leave the house. While all this was taking place, Dennis maintained an attitude of utter astonishment and pretended to be shocked and disgusted at his neighbour's behaviour.

Another time, Dennis wanted to find out how an enemy of his, Michael Dan Fahy would react in a crisis situation. They were both cutting turf near Lough Na Hinch and Dennis jumped into the water. He called out 'Help!", pretending that he was drowning. Neighbours came from all directions to try to help him but his enemy remained unmoved. Dennis smiled as he heard Michael Dan say, "I'd let the good for nothing drown and bedamned to him". The 'rescue" wasn't difficult, seeing that most of the lake water is less than three feet deep and of course there was never any question of Dennis being in danger of drowning anyway.

NUTS AT HALLOWE'EN

'Trick or treat" games played by groups of adults called 'Brideogs" were very common in Dennis's era. These groups would take gates and other objects from their bases at Halloween and would transfer them to other locations long distances away. They would direct most of their activities against those householders who failed to treat them. Dennis and his friends took part in one of these events once. A man by the name of Morrissey lived nearby and he invariably refused to contribute to the Brideogs. Furthermore, he threatened dire consequences on anyone who would dare to interfere with his property. When Dennis and company arrived at Morrisseys, they found the gate closed and there was a piece of string tied to it which was intended to alert the owner should anyone attempt to remove it. Dennis spotted the string and by untying it carefully, he and his friends were able to remove it without being detected. When the gate had been removed, Dennis gave a violent tug to the string and dived for cover. It was just as well that he did so because Morrissey's response was instantaneous. He came to the window with a double barrel shotgun and discharged two rounds in the direction of the intruders. Dennis and his friends were unharmed but it took the owner quite some time to recover his gate, which had been placed in an inaccessible paddock about two miles away.

On a second Brideog expedition Dennis and company discovered an inebriate lying insensible near the public house. They converted a gate which they had taken into a kind of stretcher and used it to take the drunken man about a mile and a half along the road. They found a house whose owner had gone visiting and managed to gain entry to it. They deposited their "passenger" on the bed and exited quickly before the owner returned. When the householder came home he was startled to hear loud snores emanating from his bedroom. He challenged his intruder who was totally oblivious of his situation and the unfortunate man was forced to bid a hasty retreat much to the amusement of Dennis and his fellow conspirators.

One of Dennis's pranks miscarried and could have been quite disastrous. Dances were being held occasionally at the parochial hall and these were frowned upon by the Parish Priest who lived close to the hall. The patrons were sometimes boisterous and the clergyman didn't like to be disturbed. Whenever there was a dance he would be on the alert and if things became too noisy he would not hesitate to clear the hall. Dennis knew this and one night he closed the gate in front of the hall and then gave a loud rap at the Priest's door. The latter responded by going straight to the hall and when he appeared, there was a massive exodus. The revellers didn't expect the gate~ to be closed and in the confusion some of them, including Dennis's son, Paddy, were crushed against the gate. No one was seriously injured but Paddy Flynn retained a souvenir of his father's prank in the form of a scar on his forehead which remained with him for the rest of his life.

LIKE FATHER LIKE SON

Dennis's son, Paddy, was sent to fetch a bottle of whiskey for Father Naughton. When he had bought it he got a second bottle which he filled with water and he dropped this on the ground and broke it in sight of the priest. The latter took pity on him and gave him the price of another bottle. This meant that Paddy and his friends were free to share the first container of whiskey among themselves.

Another time he invited an elderly bachelor who had been cutting turf near Lough na Hinch to accompany him on a boat trip on the lake. The invitation was accepted and when they were near the islet in the middle of the lake Paddy said, "Now that you're here, stand up and have a good look at the scenery". When the man stood up, Paddy gave a heave to the boat and his passenger fell headlong into the water. Even though the water wasn't deep, it took Paddy, Dennis and one or two helpers to rescue the bachelor and get him back into the boat again. The man's clothes were soaking and he attempt- ed to dry them by hanging them on bushes. It was bad enough having to remain semi - naked in the bog on a chilly day but to add to his discomfort, the Flynn's continued to draw the attention of passers - by to the man's predicament.
Ladies nearby were told to come and "see poor Mike who was nearly drained. They rushed to the spot immediately. They were unprepared for the sight that met their eyes. The partly clad Mike was shivering in his underclothes while his shirt and pants fluttered wildly in the midday breeze".
Going home was out of the question since he lived more than four miles from Lough na Hinch. So the poor bachelor had to endure cold and embarrassment while he waited for his clothes to dry. For some strange reason Flynn's boat trips in the lake

were never quite as popular after this incident.

THE LAST LAUGH

There are many other stories concerning the exploits of Dennis Flynn but these are too numerous to mention. Despite his fondness for devilment he was not malicious. Most of his pranks were harmless and very often even the victims would have a good laugh at their misfortunes at a later date. He had a great sense of humour and had no objection to playing the role of "fall-guy" whenever the occasion demanded. He was a big man and could laugh heartily at his own misfortunes. Dennis and his contemporaries relied on their own resources for entertainment. Though his era lacked conveniences and the hustle and bustle of the modern world, these were more than compensated for by their ingenuity and sense of humour. Harvest time for country folk is a time of celebration and characters like Dennis Flynn guaranteed that there was just as much fun and excitement in rural Ireland in the long dark nights of the cold seasons as there was in the warm, sunny days of summer.

CHAPTER SIX

THE MEN FROM CONNEMARA

In the past, hundreds of Connemara men travelled the length and breadth of Ireland in search of work. 'Na spalpini' or 'cunnies', as they were called were a familiar and thriving species in the forties, fifties and sixties. The type of work they did included farming operations of all kinds, especially thatching, beet thinning and grain harvesting but their services were in greatest demand during turf-cutting and potato digging periods. There were many different kinds of characters but the one thing they had in common was a willingness to work. To compensate for this they liked to lubricate themselves internally with a generous supply of dark frothy liquid at regular intervals.

The treatment they received varied. Some were well looked after by their employers but many of them were harshly treated and regarded the public house as the only refuge to which they could retire during their leisure time. Hiring fairs for Connemara workers were held in various centres especially during spring and harvest. People from East Galway travelled to Athenry where 'cunnies' could be seen standing around the square to be hired after Sunday mass. Over the years many stories and legends have been based on the lives of these Connemara workmen.

Some farmers tried to enrich themselves by squeezing the last ounce of labour out of their unfortunate employees. There is a story told about one such person who used to force his men to dig potatoes by the light of a storm lantern. However these same workers got their revenge by slicing the newly dug 'spuds', thus obliging the farmer to abandon his unnatural

working hours in favour of a more civilised rota. Unfair practices were not all on the one side, of course. There are many stories of spalpeens taking advantage of widows or elderly people by claiming payment for work which was badly done or in some cases, not done at all. It has also been claimed that some workmen compiled a list of employers, noting how each employer
treated his or her workmen. This kind of information was probably very useful to them and could help to protect them from some of the more unscrupulous employers.

As if to confirm the theory of long working hours they had to endure, there is a yarn about two workmen who were asked by a friend to describe where they were staying. They said they couldn't possibly do this because they used to set out for the working field before dawn and didn't return until after dark, therefore they had never seen the place in daylight.

There are several names of Connemara men that are remembered in East Galway, These include Jim Mullen, Padraig Delaney, Tom Connolly, Festy
Fitzpatrick, Padraig Conroy, Tomas O'Maille, Jim O'Donnell and Padraig Derrane However there is one name that stands out above all others and that is Jimmy Joyce.

JIMMY JOYCE

Jimmy was about 5'8" tall, of average build, with dark hair which he retained right throughout his life. He was a hard working man who began work early and was capable of performing a wide range of manual activities. The job he liked best and probably earned most money at was turf-cutting.

Slaning the turf, two wheelers drawing it out from him, a fire on the turf bank to boil the kettle, a bog hole without water in it then Jimmy would work to his heart's content and the householder would have a year's supply of turf at the end of the week.

Heavy manual work never presented Jimmy with any difficulty. The greatest problem he faced was the English language or rather his lack of it. He could never quite utilise conventional forms of expression in order to convey his ideas. Instead he relied mainly on Gaelic idioms, often with very amusing results.

One day he wanted to know how much turf a farmer intended to cut and he phrased the question in the following manner: "Tell me boss iss she much long for cut?" Another day he had been sowing a garden and was on his way to the public house at 11.30 am when he was greeted by a neighbour.

"Nice day Jimmy", said the neighbour.

"She wass a nice day", said Jimmy who had begun work that morning around 6.00 that morning.

Although Jimmy owned a bicycle he usually confined himself to the Gurteen, Ballymacward, Menlough and Caltra districts. Once he worked in Ballygar and apparently didn't do too well. In order to show his displeasure at the treatment he received , he vowed that his appearances there would be as rare as those of the cuckoo. Often in mid-conversation, especially when he had a few drinks on board, he would utter the expression, "Cuckoo Ballygar", much to the bewilderment of his listeners.

Like most of his fellow workers, Jimmy would work for lower wages during off peak periods like the winter. Spalpeens were happy to do the foddering and such work in return for their keep and the price of a few pints. A substantial increase was expected when spring arrived, and if this was
not forthcoming, then they would move to anther area in search of better paid work. Jimmy had been staying and working for and elderly lady on this basis and when Spring arrived she asked him to continue working for her for a few more weeks.
His reply was, "I will stay alright but I will have to be rising upon you". Some local wits claimed that the woman retorted, "Well Jimmy, I was thinking of cutting you".

ON THE ROAD

Whether on his bicycle or slaning, Jimmy invariably wore a peaked cap and a brown suit. One Gurteen farmer used to say "Toppin' man Jimmy Joyce, wears brown clothes and drinks black porter".

In between working stints and drinking Jimmy managed to find occasional opportunities for
romance. These romantic interludes tended to be of short duration. Once he was describing a
relationship which he had with a young lady to a Caltra farmer. Jimmy left the district where the young woman lived and the farmer said, "I suppose that finished the line Jimmy?"
"Oh, no, no, no". he replied, "She still letter to me and I letter to her". On another occasion an acquaintance~once once urged Jimmy to try his luck with a lady of notoriously loose morals. He dismissed the idea on the spot with the comment,

"Yowl. I not be seen with colleen! She give belly to other mans".

Jimmy tended to be careless in health matters. He was inspired by the belief that if he contracted tuberculosis and had to be hospitalised in a sanitarium that he would receive a regular weekly allowance. It is not surprising therefore that Jimmy spent many nights sleeping rough during his odyssey in East Galway. As well as being a spalpeen himself, Jimmy also claimed to have a sister who did similar work for English farmers. One curious individual wanted to know what work she did and the reply was "Threshing"

"What kind of threshing does she do?"

"Oats no barley you fool" was Jimmy's reply.

Despite his linguistic peculiarities there was never any problem understanding him. He usually embellished his conversation with winks, nods, manual and facial expressions of various kinds. He was impatient with those who were slow to understand him but when the roles were reversed he wouldn't hesitate to call out, "What's it saying?"

Despite his fondness for drink he avoided brawls and other disreputable conduct. He nearly always had a smile and a cheerful greeting for those he encountered. Even though he was an affable person, he could be quite critical of those of whom he didn't approve.

"She was nice girl but hadn't much smart" was his comment on one young lady.

"Arra. That fellow give bits of cats for dinner was how he described another stingy farmer.

"He be a scrow of the worst kind", was his verdict on another of his employers.

Jimmy was afraid of lightening and wouldn't work out of doors whenever there was thundery weather. He was in bed one night during a thunderstorm. He woke up to see a blinding flash of light followed by a loud peal of thunder. There was a radio in the house and he knew that there was some relationship between it and lightening. Almost paralysed by fear himself, he gave a loud roar in the direction of the farmer's bedroom.

"God's sake someone take the buachaill out of the shee". meaning that somebody should disconnect the radio.

One of the most amusing stories concerning Jimmy is his description of a puncture which

occurred in Tample in the parish of Gurteen. He described the event in his own inimitable style.

"I pump her upon Ned Burke and I pump her again upon Molly Mannion. I wass goin' down road and she did let shoot like tay-bag. My God, sez I, What time she did let shoot., I look at front roller (wheel) and there wasn't puff breeze in her. I have Warwick pump and Dunlop tube and I afraid to mix air".

Jimmy didn't like to stay too long in any one place. "A rolling rock she grow no moss", was one of his expressions. Sometimes he would quit early on a Saturday to buy a tyre for his bicycle. When he would return the following day without having replaced the tyre, a curious farmer might want to know the reason. "I meet mo chara Padraig and we go to tap room. The black cow (porter), she swallow the price of roller." In Other words he and his companion drank the money with which he intended to buy the tyre. His favourite song and his philosophy coincided. The name of the song was:- An Cruiscin Lan

On another occasion Jimmy was carting some farmyard manure or or 'top dress' as it was sometimes called. As he was turning into the field the wheel of the cart got stuck in the gatepost. After some struggling and cursing Jimmy eventually freed the wheel and then brought the horse and cart into the field. He then ran back to the post and gave it three or four hefty kicks before returning to his work.

Jimmy Joyce unfortunately is no longer with us. He passed away in the previous decade having succumbed to the disease which he had hoped would provide him with a ticket to the 'good life'. 'Cunnies' or spalpeens are now a rare sight in rural Ireland. Dennis O'Mahony from Cork was probably one of the last travelling workmen to be seen in this area. Social conditions have improved greatly since Jimmy Joyce's time. Connemara men no longer have to suffer the hardship that Jimmy and his colleagues had to endure. Hiring fairs in Athenry and other areas have long since disappeared. The' cunnies' are almost a forgotten breed and a few remember the tremendous contribution they made to life in rural Ireland.

Machinery has replaced them workwise but nothing can replace the humour and colour which they contributed to rural communities throughout Ireland. They were tough men who experienced more thorns than roses in if so let's hope that their thirst for work and alcohol has been fully satisfied in their eternal resting place.

The following verses are dedicated to Jimmy and his friends:

THE MAN FROM CONNEMARA

I

He worked the hours of daylight,
He ploughed the land by dawn,
He knows what cold and hunger are,
His clothes were often torn.
Though his life was filled with hardship,
His courage we admire,
The man from Connemara,
Who sought his daily hire.

II

He was called to sow potatoes,
He came to thin the beet,
'Twas he who set the turnips
And thatched with straw so neat. He slaned the marshy boglands, And
got black turf for the fire, The man from Connemara,
Who earned us daily hire.

III

The work was often tedious, And the pace was rarely slow, The food was
sometimes
scanty, Yet his heart was never low. The crops were often weedy, The
roads were filled
with mire, But the man from Connemara,
Enjoyed his daily hire

Iv

No more the country farmers, Will come to Athenry,
To hire the travelling spalpeens, Who happen to come by.
He'll no longer bring his knapsack, To settle by the fire,
Or quench his thirst on Sundays, As he rested from his hire

V

His day of glory's over now, There's no hiring anymore,
The horse and plough we all allow, Belong to days of yore.
But his deeds will be remembered, His fame will not expire, The man
from Connemara,
Who sought his daily hire.

CHAPTER SEVEN

SPARKLING STORIES FROM PAT

Pat Kenny was a tall, broad shouldered farmer who lived in Cappalusk. His strength matched his appearance and he worked hard to make a living on a small holding of poor quality land. Like other strong men, Pat's services were constantly in demand especially for difficult farming chores such as dosing strong cattle or killing pigs. "God spare you the health", or a small payment in kind was the usual reward for this kind of work. However, small financial returns didn't prevent Pat from making his services available whenever they were required. As well as being a good neighbour, Pat was a gifted storyteller. He had a vast repertoire of stories and when he visited neighbouring houses, these never failed to delight his audiences. He could speak authoritatively on many subjects and his personal involvement in some of the events which he described gave them an authenticity and an appeal which aroused the spirit of curiosity in his listeners. His stories dealt with local, national and international events.

A SPEEDY EXIT

For many young people, Pat was the embodiment of the traditional hero, being tall, strong and athletic and a determined seeker of truth and fair play. Pat Kenny's era was one of social upheaval and widespread political unrest. He was a stanch supporter of the United Irish League and made no attempt to hide his dislike of English rule in Ireland. This attitude of his was probably responsible for several skirmishes he had with the law.

Despite these he was never imprisoned for his seditious activities. On one occasion he engaged in a fracas with police after a political meeting in Ballymacward. At the end of the scuffle a constable tried to arrest him but Pat escaped by giving him a hard blow on the head. After hitting the policeman and knocking him to the ground, Pat took to his heels and was immediately pursued by another member of the force. After he had run two miles, Pat was lost sight of by his pursuer. The latter asked a passer-by if he had seen the fugitive. The passer-by replied, "I 'm afraid your Quarry has long since gone to ground.". The disheartened officer gave up the chase and Kenny reached his destination safely. Fortunately for him the policeman didn't know his name or where he lived.

His athleticism served him well on another occasion when he and a friend were chased by some soldiers after they had disrupted a recruiting meeting. Pat and his companions quickly outran the soldiers and they both reached home safely, having travelled several miles of rough, cross-country terrain. These adventures evoked great admiration among those fortunate enough to hear them being told by the main character who was involved in them.

GETTING THE POINT

What made Pat's story-telling different was the fact that he used to give practical illustrations of some of the events he was describing. In order to show how he had subdued a quarrelsome opponent, he would sometimes grab hold of a listener and use him as a guinea pig. Very often this led to amusing results. The unfortunate listener would have to remain in a passive position while the author proceeded to demonstrate how he had won a particular fight. To make matters worse, other members of the audience would usually try to make the "guinea pig" laugh by performing amusing antics behind Pat's back. Woe betide the unfortunate individual should he show any sign of mirth. If this were to happen he might well be at the receiving end of Pat's powerful pugilistic skill.

FOLKLORE AND FANTASY

As mentioned already, Pat seemed to have an infinite store of myths and legends. For example, he could~give an enthralling account of a strange dark dog that was supposed to be seen late at night at Scarrys Well or a ghostly maiden whom it was claimed could be seen combing her long, dark hair at Creeraun Gate. Other legends described haunted houses. Pat used to encourage audience participation by inviting his listeners to suggest possible explanations for the hauntings. He used to tell equally intriguing stories about people who suddenly found themselves trapped in locations that should have been familiar to them. It appeared that no matter how hard they tried to escape from these locations, they were unable to do so until a long period of time had elapsed. Individuals who suffered in this way were never able to give a satisfactory explanation for their experiences.

One of Pat's eeriest stories was about the time he had been returning from Ahascragh in the early hours of the morning. He had spent all that day drying grain at the local mill. As he travelled homewards he felt like a smoke and just then he noticed a light in a house some distance off the road. He decided he would ask the householder for a coal to kindle his pipe. As he reached the door the light went out. He knocked on the door and called out "I just want a coal to light my pipe".
There was no response. He knocked again and repeated his request. Still no response. He continued to knock on the door and suddenly a weird looking bearded face appeared and

pressed itself close to the window pane and stared menacingly at him . He made no further attempt to enter the house and he returned quickly to the public road and continued his journey home. Several times he
thought he was being followed but on each occasion when he stopped there was nothing to be seen or heard.
It was only as he crossed a small stream near home that the feeling of being followed finally left him. In folklore it is a strongly held belief that evil spirits are reluctant to cross water and

Pat's experience on this occasion would appear to offer some credence to the belief.

The Kennys

PAT AND MARIA PICTURED AT HOME IN CAPPALUSK

THE STAG OF NAUL

One of the all time favourites at the fireside was a well known saga familiar to students of folklore as the Stag of Naul. It concerned a Frenchman who arrived in Naul (North Co. Dublin) in 1798 looking for work. He claimed to be a French soldier lately escaped from prison and although the rebels were suspicious at first, eventually he gained their confidence and was accepted into the United Irishmen. No one seems to know what the Frenchman's name was but he soon became known as Vive La because of his fondness for using that expression. One day, Vive La visited Balbriggan and was spotted by a "United" man entering the British Army barracks there. A close watch was kept on Vive La from that day forward. Three volunteers were given the task of ensuring that he did not travel to Balbriggan again. Vive La soon realised he was being watched and attempted to slip away unnoticed one day. He was intercepted and taken to a barn which normally sheltered labourers. There was a heavy downpour during the night and Vive La escaped from the barn while his captors slept.

At sunrise, three armed men set off in pursuit. This proved to be a most dramatic affair. The hunters thought they had their quarry caught several times but Vive La outwitted them on each occasion. Cornered at last, he jumped off a cliff. Although badly shaken, he survived and remained hidden for some time in an effort to convince his pursuers that he had been killed. His pursuers however continued to watch and soon realised that Vive La was still alive. He was finally captured, questioned and killed at Naul Bridge. One of those involved then stole the pants worn by Vive La. This almost cost him his life. A seamstress who was friendly with British soldiers recognised the trousers

47

as one she had mended for Vive La. The man and his two companions were arrested and charged with murder. Leonard McNally, the brilliant lawyer who later betrayed many of the leaders of the United Irishmen, defended those accused of
the killing. In court, McNally asked to have the garment in question handed to him. He then asked the seamstress if she had any doubt about it being the garment she had repaired. She replied that she had not. McNally then dropped the breeches carelessly as if intending it to rest on the edge of the table but it struck the edge and fell on the ground. The lawyer apologised, stooped and arose breeches in hand. He then threw the garment towards the seamstress and ask her to examine it as closely as possible. She did so. She said, "Upon my oath, this patch is my own work and I have no doubt about it". "Good", said McNally as he bent down and produced the original breeches from
under the table. "Here are the breeches you have already sworn to which I have interchanged with those which you now hold in your hand". The court had no option but to find the accused not guilty. McNally said to his clients, "Next time you hunt a stag to death, take my advice and don't flay him". Who can be surprised if our palms sweated and our pulses raced as we listened to such tales.

THE LONG ROAD

Pat enjoyed walking. He travelled on foot on numerous occasions to markets, fairs an to visit relatives. Once a member of the family needed a doctor and Pat set off at 6.30 a.m. to fetch the doctor. He reached the doctor's house in Athenry at 9 o'clock having travelled ten miles through bog, field and forest. He returned later in the morning and after a brief respite began his day's work on the farm.

Fireside story tellers tellers are a rare species nowadays and as Pat himself would say, "More 's the pity". Even though he spoke English, he used many Irish idioms in his conversation. On entering a house he used to greet those present with, "God save all here" or if the people were engaged in some chore "God bless the work". Foul language was not part of his vocabulary and his strongest "swear" words were "Be crimers" or "Be damn but". He was a healthy individual who rarely, if ever, needed medical attention. He and his friends enjoyed wholesome home-made food. His favourite thirst quencher, especially when working in the meadow, was oatmeal at the bottom of a can containing pure spring water.

Pat was ready to express himself fearlessly at all times. He expected others to have equally high standards and wouldn't accept "black-sliding" or double dealing from anyone. He and his wife spent many happy years together in their thatched cottage rearing their family. Though they didn't possess much material wealth they were always ready to share what they had with others. Pat disapproved of bullying and never allowed oppressors to go unchallenged.

Strangely enough, he often succeeded in overpowering those who were physically stronger than he was through the intelligent use of his skill and agility. He didn't believe in seeking trouble but when it came his way, he was ready, willing and able to deal with it. One of the things which annoyed Pat most was that he had to deliver turf to Daly's of Dunsandle.

The Dalys were unpopular landlords and all tenants of theirs had to supply them with firewood if they wished to retain possession of their holdings: The latter were delighted when this custom came to an end. This happened when Daly's estate was taken over by the Land Commission and redivided among the tenant farmers.

Here is an alliterative curse which indicates the level of hostility with which the family was regarded: The Devil double damn Denis Daly and his descendants of Dunsandle Demesne. Gradually the aristocracy were obliged to give ground to the peasantry and even though money was scarce, rustics had an opportunity for the first time to manage their farms free from the oppressive influence of the landed gentry. This freedom was a just reward for Pat and his contemporaries who had laboured unceasingly so that they might get a reasonable degree of control over their own destinies.

We can be justly proud of the part that Pat and his comrades played in the struggle for social and political reform. The memory of this proud, independent individual lingers long after his passing. He had an outgoing, friendly nature and a tremendous zest for life. Pat used his talents to entertain and educate the community. His storytelling and his heroic deeds are still fondly remembered in his native parish.

CHAPTER EIGHT

ST. KERRILL'S HOLY VOWS AND SOME UNHOLY VOWS

Clonkeen kerrill - the delightful meadow of Kerrill, was one of the coarbs or seven main territories of Ui Maine. The others were Clonfert, Killimian, Kiltullagh, Killicomedon, Camaghbride and Clontuskert. Clonkeenkerrill was once a parish in its own right and contained the town lands of Shanballard, Shanballymore Shanballyeeshal, Sheeaun, Temple and Gortnalone. In the past there was a two teacher primary school located there also. At present the village has about a dozen houses, two buildings which were once used as a school houses and a cemetery plot containing the ruins of an old abbey. This abbey is about one mile north of Gurteen Church and about six miles south east of Monivea.

The abbey is thought to mark the site of and earlier church founded by St Kerrill and is situated on a small hill.People from a wide radius chose Clonkeenkerrill Cemetery as their final resting-place.

THE MAN HIMSELF

St. Kerrill is a figure stretching back into the mists of antiquity and information about his life is difficult to obtain or verify. Many followers claim he lived in the fifth century around the time of St. Patrick, while others claimed that he lived until about 693 A.D. Tradition suggests that he was born in Donegal and that he was a nephew of St.Columcille and a son of the King of Ossory. These, people believed that he worked on the mission fields of Scotland with his uncle before returning to Ireland. After returning to his native country, he is thought to have worked in various western countries before finally establishing his church Clonkeenkerrill. Tradition also claims that Kerill was an ascetic famed for his unselfishness and works of piety wherever he travelled.

FROM CHURCH TO MONASTERY

The church that Kerrill built would have been relatively small and it wasn't until centuries later that the monastery, the ruins of which can be seen today, was actually built. In 1435 the bishop gave John and David Mulcairrol the present site with permission to rebuild the temple into a Monastery. In 1453 the Pope gave David Mulcairrol authority to convert the house from the 3rd to the 1st order of St. Francis. The monastery housed a number of brothers and continued to exist until 1618 when it was abandoned or destroyed for some unknown reason. It is thought that there is an underground passage leading from the Abbey to a nearby hillside. However this has never been explored. Some people have suggested that it may contain chalices or other valuable church property hidden there at some stage by the Franciscan Brothers.

THE ABBEY RUINS TODAY

The site today contains a lancet arched window, a Gothic window, a tomb and a number of wall memorials. One inscription refers to Edmond Kelly, doctor of Sorbonne and vicar of the diocese who is buried there. He was consecrated Bishop in 1718 and was probably appointed Bishop of Clonfert in 1733 when a vacancy occurred in that Diocese. To the left, some distance from the entrance, there is a slab of stone known as Kerrill's Bed. Many parishioners rest the coffins of their dead on this slab before interment takes place. No one is quite sure how this custom originated but one source suggests that it goes back to the time when people from the district delivered their dead to the monks to be buried. The coffins were probably brought to the door of the monastery and left on a slab before being handed over to the monks who would then complete the burial process.

REMEMBERING KERRILL

The 13th of June marks the Feast of Kerrill and is still celebrated in the parish. Up to recent times parishioners abstained from. manual work of all kinds on this day and would attend a special Mass also. Later in the day people would travel to Gortnalone, which is about 3 rniles, from Clonkeenkerrill, to recite prayers and to collect water from St. Kerrill's Well. There was a strong belief that this holy water protected one from the danger of lightening. It is claimed by some local people that as a result of Kerrill's intercession, no-one in the parish of Gurteen has been, or ever will be, killed by lightening.The belief was strengthened in the seventies. A chimney stack in Creeraun was struck during a severe thunderstorm but the occupants of the house remained untouched. After devotions at the well, older people would retire to their homesteads while the young and the young at heart would prepare for a night's dancing and revelry in the local hall. Dances on St. Kerrill's night were well attended and attracted people from miles around. Nowadays people still attend Mass on the feast day and a festival is held annually on the week-endof the 13th of June. There is usually a sponsored walk to St. Kerrill's well and a number of functions, including discos and a party for senior citizens. These are held in the local lounge. In 1993 a magazine to commemorate Kerrill's death was published and a Mayoral election was organised to raise funds locally.

A GRAVE FAMILY ROW

The cemetery on the grounds of St. Kerrill's Abbey is the final resting place for hundreds of people in Gurteen and surrounding areas. There is one curious custom associated with this cemetery. No-one is ever buried there on a Monday! Tradition explains this custom by relating it to a dispute which is said to have taken place between Kerrill and his brother St. Connell of Kilconnell. One version of the story claims that the two disagreed over the use of a hammer or building implement. It is unclear whether it was a dispute about ownership or whether it was a question of their wanting to use it at the same time. Another source suggests a different reason for this "saintly"disagreement. It states that Connell invited Kerrill to visit him on a certain Monday. Kerrill not wishing to go for some reason excused himself by saying he wished to attend a funeral. Connell is reported to have responded by saying that there would always be a funeral in Clonkeenkerril cemetery on a Monday. Kerrill for his part part prophesised that blood would

be spilled at every fair in Kilconnell. As a result of the intercession of Kerrill, in a place of human, it was said that a bird
would die instead and some people have said that the bird in
question was a starling. There is no way of ascertaining whether
or not either of these predictions came true. As far as Kilconnell
is concerned, fairs have long since ceased to be held there, so
therefore it is impossible that blood should be spilled at them.
As for Clonkeenkerrill, no-one has ever reported finding an
unusually large number of dead birds there on Mondays or any
other day of the week. Despite this, very few ever risked
incurring the wrath of Kerril by interring their loved ones on a
Monday. On one occasion a farmer from Cloncagh parish
ignored the custom and buried a relative there on the forbidden
day. It was said that the person in question later suffered from
serious health problems and that he also lost a number of valuable cattle. One way or another no other challenger has come
forward to repeat the experience within the past twenty years.

A ROAD WITHOUT END

Another story concerns a road which was begun in
Clonkeenkerrill and crossed the nearby Coolough bog in the
direction of Ballymacward and Kilconnell. There is evidence
that stones for this project were quarried locally. One of the
stone pits in question was closed in about fifteen years
ago. Also when some bogland was being drained several trail-
er loads of stones were removed from one field. Large quantities of stones are seldom found in bogs, therefore this would
suggest that they were brought there for the purpose of roadmaking. The road itself was never completed but there is what
appears to be the outline of such a road crossing the Coolock
bog.

St. Kerrill: Man or Myth?

As with most famous characters, stories and legends concerning St. Kerrill abound. No trace of Kerrill can be found in the calendar of saints and many sceptics query his very existence. At best they insist that he was just a holy monk or abbot who has no great miracles or works of piety to his credit. At the other end of the scale there are those who place him on a par with St. Patrick and many claim that he had as his ancestors the ancient high Kings of Ireland. Wherever the truth lies between these conflicting theories, the fact remains that Kerrill has had a long and powerful influence on the people of Clonkeenkerrill and its surroundings. What is even more extraordinary is the fact that St. Kerrill is known and revered outside Ireland.

A few years ago the curate in Gurteen received a letter from Scotland seeking more information about the Saint and his birth place. Such was the piety of the mighty man that the people of Inverness built a church dedicated to his memory sometime in the thirteenth century.

ST. KERRILL STILL REIGNS

Over the years debates and discussions about St Kerrill have taken place in the workplace and by the firesides of Clonkeenkerrill and the surrounding parishes. Was he a holy saint who had the power to protect his parishioners from the destructive power of lightening over the centuries? Had he the power to punish them if they contravened the custom of non burial in Clonkeenkerrill cemetery on a Monday? We may never know the answers to these questions but I think one thing is obvious. Although many of the stories and legends surrounding the great man nay be far fetched or fanciful, we cannot dismiss St. Kerrill as a figment of the imagination.

Despite the growth of materialism, devotion to him is still

strong in the area. St. Kerril's influence on his parishioners seems destined to extend to the twenty first century. Instead of diminishing, interest in him has grown with the passage of time. Wherever you find an Irishman with the Christian name of Kerrill you can be sure that either he or his ancestors hailed from Clonkeenkerrill or its neighbourhood.

KILLUANE

Killuane Churchyard is two miles from Clonkeenkerrill. This building was erected by a holy man named named Dubhan several centuries ago. The walled area of the cemetery measures twenty by thirty yards approximately but the plot may have been larger at one stage because skeletons and other body parts were recovered in a field across the road. This road could not have existed when the church was built and once there was a mark in the field which could have corresponded to a cemetery fence. The church building or monastery seemed to have contained two chambers and there is a small window in the east wall with two slabs on edge, touching at the top and forming a pointed head. There is also a small doorway in the west wall with a large flat stone forming the head. The cemetery is small and funerals there are rare - perhaps one burial every four or five years. The ruins are situated about four hundred feet over sea level. There is fertile soil and a good deal of trees in the area and there is a commanding view of the surrounding countryside from the churchyard.

KILLUANE CHURCHYARD

St. Kerrill's Hymn

I

Hail, O' Patron sainted Kerrill,
Hear our voices raised to you,
Guardian of our homes and parish
On this day we ask of you,
That the faith which thou has planted
Never shall grow dim or old;
But as lightning bursts through
    darkness
May it scatter demons bold.

II

Long Ago in age of Darkness
When the world~forgot it's God,
Saint and hero, holy Martyr
Taught the Faith on Erin's sod.
Sword and famine, wars,
Dread thunder bursting oe'r.
Our land has been
But the altar lamp kept
Burning in the Abbey at Clonkeen.

III

See us kneeling round thy altar,
Hands and voices joined in prayer.
All we long for, hope for, wish for
We commit them to thy care.
For our parents, homes and parish,
We will pray this blessed day
That the faith which kept Kerrill
planted
May drive danger far away.

IV

And today, in our hour of triumph
Where the wiles of Satan fail,
We shall deck another Altar
And with hymn the Lord we hail.
We shall praise his goodness and
mercy,
In the struggles of the past,
And with sainted Kerrill pleading
We shall share his crown at last.

58

CHAPTER NINE

AND BARTLEY BEATS THE DEVIL-
THE EXPLOITS OF AN IRISH ROGUE

Bartley Loughnane lived in the village of Lisheen. He was such an extraordinary individual that people who didn't know him would find it very difficult to believe some of the things he did. By profession he was a farmer but he specialised in cheating and he nearly always managed to get the better of his antagonists. The following is a brief selection of Bartley's escapades.

We begin with the Bank Manager in Ballinasloe. Bartley decided to take out a loan and as he was herding for Mr. Rothwell a landowner-cum-businessman, he named him as guarantor. Mr. Rothwell had no hesitation in securing the money for him. The loan was repaid promptly and sometime later, Mr. Rothwell acted as guarantor for a second loan. Once more the money was quickly repaid and the manager was very pleased with his new customer. Mr. Rothwell was unavailable on a third occasion, when a new loan was required but by now the manager felt he could trust Bartley and gave him the money on his personal warranty. This sum of money, which was larger than the previous ones, was never repaid.

A Ballygar merchant suffered a similar fate. Bartley visited him early one day and selected a bicycle which he said he would buy later that day. There was a fair in the town and when he had sold his cattle, he would be able to buy the bike. In the meantime he would have to walk some distance to meet his son-in-law who was bringing the cattle to town. The merchant took pity on him and seeing that he intended to buy it anyway, told him to take it away with him. Bartley accepted the offer and the

59

owner didn't see him or the bike ever again.

There are numerous accounts of shopkeepers providing household goods without receiving any payment for them. On one occasion Bartley had a cartload of groceries and was about to pay for them. Just at the critical moment his brother-in-law arrived. He had just bought a calf and needed more money to pay for the animal. Bartley told the shopkeeper to take back the merchandise because he would have to give money to his brother-in-law. The shopkeeper insisted on his taking the goods and needless to say the debt was not honoured.

On another occasion one of Bartley's daughters was about to be married. He killed a number of sheep belonging to Mr. Rothwell and these were used for the wedding banquet. A local farmer had a habit of allowing his dogs out for an early morning run. Bartley claimed that the dogs killed the sheep and demanded compensation from the farmer. The latter was obliged to pay or risk the possibility of legal action being taken against him.

Although his in-laws collaborated with him in many of his schemes, they were not immune from exploitation by him either. A son-in-law required concrete stakes once and Barley told him that the landlord was selling some but didn't want to publicise he fact. He advised the son-in-law to come in his cart late at night and to cover the bottom of the vehicle with straw to prevent the stakes hitting against one another or making too much noise. This was duly done. Bartley sat in the rear of the cart and dropped the stakes silently on the grass as he drove along. When the son-in-law examined the cart the next day all he had was a pile of straw. The stakes which he had paid for had completely disappeared.

Another family of his in-laws suffered a much more severe blow. Dowries were a common feature of life in those days.

Bartley's second daughter was about to get married and he was expected to give a substantial sum of money to his future in-laws. He visited the farm where she was to live and pronounced himself satisfied with its condition. He then demanded to see the deeds of ownership These were produced. There was one problem however. He had left his glasses at home and although several spectacles were offered to him, he was unable to read the documents. Finally it was agreed that he could take them with him and read them at his leisure Bartley took them to the local bank and obtained a loan producing the deeds as security. He used this money to pay the dowry. The unfortunate in-laws found that they were responsible to the bank for the loan and this must have been a rare, if not the only case of a family providing funds for a dowry to itself.

Bartley didn't seem to worry about the consequences of his actions. Even when legal proceedings were taken against him, he still came through with flying colours. There are few records of plaintiffs taking successful cases against him. On one occasion occasion he went up to a merchant who was suing him and shook hands with him. The merchant did not recognise him as he had grown a beard since he last saw him. When the case began, Bartley produced witnesses to prove that the merchant did not know him at all and that he was suing the wrong man. The court agreed and case was dismissed.

One creditor was thwarted when he attempted to track down Bartley at home. He met the man he was looking for but failed to recognise him. Bartley gave such a description of his own character that the creditor decided to cut his losses and counted himself lucky to have got off so lightly. Another shopkeeper wasn't so lucky. Bartley was on his way to a forge shortly after his mother's death. He was stopped by the shopman who told him that his mother owed him money.

"Is that so?" he asked. "I never knew she dealt with you at all. Sure if I knew she was shopping here I'd be dealing here myself as well". He paid the bill but got more goods on credit and left the shopkeeper with a much larger unpaid bill.

At that time, people who were mentally ill were not held responsible for their debts. Our hero was aware of this and decided to go "insane" to avoid paying his creditors. While he was in this condition he was fastened securely by ropes to a bed and his wife and neighbours attended to him.

One Sunday morning he was thought to have "recovered" from his "madness" and his wife told his neighbours to "Let him loose to me." On being released the patient ran out of the house in his underclothes and set off across the fields for Joyce's of Corgary a few miles away. Joyce, who was a landlord, found Bartley fingering a gun dangerously in the hallway and tried to pacify him until help arrived. He also gave him an expensive suit of clothes to make him "decent". He was then brought to St. Brigid's Mental Hospital in Ballinasloe. Psychiatrists could find nothing wrong with him and he was released shortly afterwards. His return to "normality" was uneventful except for the fact that on his way home from the mental hospital he "lifted" a brand new knapsack sprayer which had been left unattended on a headland by the unsuspecting owner.

Bartley didn't confine his nefarious dealings to business people or professionals. Neighbours were well used to hay, turf and other farm produce disappearing mysteriously whenever Bartley was around. When they saw him coming to visit with a rope in his possession, they presumed that he intended to steal hay. Likewise, when they saw him coming with a bag, they deduced that he meant to take turf He usually did the opposite of what was expected from him and he seemed to be able to escape detection no matter how vigilant property owners were.

STICKING TO HIS GUNS

Agrarian unrest was rife at this lime. As he worked for a land-lord Bartley knew that this kind of activity posed a threat to his livelihood. At one stage he occupied a gatehouse belonging to the landlord. There he heard rumours of an impending attack on the landlord's property. While staying at the gate house he was visited by a sympathiser of the would-be attackers. Both men were in mid-conversation when there was a tap at the win-dow. Bartley opened it and a gun was handed in. He took the gun upstairs and returned to receive another one. Several weapons were taken by him in this manner and nothing was said while this was happening. What the visitor didn't know was that there was only one gun in question all the time. This was being taken in the window, carried upstairs and handed down to an accomplice outside. The ruse was successful. The agitators were informed that a virtual arsenal was being stored up by the landlord and they decided not to go ahead with the attack.

Although Bartley exploited his neighbours, he was ready to help them too. He lent farm implements, assisted them at calv-ing time and with the threshing. One of his favourite sayings was, "When God is on your side you can't go wrong".
God certainly appeared to favour Bartley because he was always successful in material matters at least. Neighbours generally avoided confrontation with him because they knew from experience that he was invariably victorious. They also feared reprisals. One lady who testified in court against him woke up one morning to find all her fowl killed.

All his campaigns were well planned and confirmed the belief that Bartley was a man of great ingenuity. An example of his cleverness can be seen in an incident where he placed a bet with a number of local people. This bet concerned a solicitor who lived in the area. The man in question was noted for his expensive fees and for the fact that he never gave advice free of charge. Barley placed a wager that he would get the lawyer's opinion without paying a penny. The locals felt that Barley had overstretched himself on this occasion and that the lawyer would not give his advice without a fee. Bartley set off in his pony and trap accompanied by one of those who had bet against him. They were on the road which the solicitor would travel on his way home from work. When the man's car was seen in the distance, Bartley moved to the right hand side of the road in the path of the oncoming car. The solicitor began to sound his hooter but Bartley continued on, uputurbed and the driver was obliged to stop. He was very angry and rolled down his window. Bartley called out,

"Is there something wrong Sir?"

"Do you not know that you are on the wrong side of the road, you bloody simpleton!"

"Oh thanks very much for your advice Sir", said the chancer as he proceeded to the correct side of the road. He had scored again by winning the bet having got the lawyer's opinion free of charge.

It is difficult to catalogue all of his escapades. His wife co-operated with him in the execution of many of these. Such an incident was one in which a bachelor from a distant parish kept pestering Bartley to find him a wife. Bartley agreed to produce a lady on a particular night. The bachelor made great preparations and Bartley and a female arrived at the appointed time. The "lady" in question was Bartley's wife and both she and the bachelor entertained one another in the parlour while Bartley feasted on the goodies in the kitchen. There were no subsequent meetings between the lady and the bachelor and it is not known whether the latter ever found out he had been cheated.

Another incident concerns a brush Bartley had with the law. He was returning from Ballinasloe via Kilconnell one night without a light on his bike. The attitude of policemen to matters of this kind was very strict at the time. Bartley knew that there would be a guard on duty in the village of Kilconnell so he dismounted before he arrived there. He then caught the bicycle and pushing it backwards, attempted to steer it by holding onto the saddle. When he met the guard the latter asked him what he was trying to do.

"Me son gave me his bike to bring home for him and the damn thing has me nearly killed".

The guard took pity on him, caught the bike by the handlebars and showed him how it should be steered. He made no reference to the fact that Bartley had not got a light. When Bartley was out of sight of the guard he remounted his bicycle and set out for home without further interruption.

WIN SOME, LOSE SOME

Although he had many successes there were also a few failures. He bought turf from one old lady in the parish and tried to avoid paying for it by saying he forgot to bring his money. He offered to leave his overcoat as a form of security until the payment was made. The woman rejected his offer and his son was dispatched to get the cash before he could leave with the turf.

SHEEP RUSTLING AND WOOL GATHERING

Once Bartley had to move sheep along the road for Mr. Rothwell who employed him as a herd . Rothwell had stock in two parishes and the intention was to combine the two flocks and sell them to a large sheep buyer . Bartley's son had been given the job of driving the sheep .Rothwell's son Paul was present when forty ewes were counted and set off from Mt. Bernard to Kilconnell. Bartley had instructed his own son to detach ewes from the flock at intervals . These could be collected from roadside fields later in the day and could be added to Bartleys' own herd. (There were no tags or electronic devices for identifying stock in those days). For some reason Paul Rothwell became suspicious and waited for Bartley's son in Kilconnell When he counted them there were nine animals missing . There was no option for young Loughnane but to retrace his steps and recover the "lost" sheep.

Bartley and neighbours. Bartley is the man in the centre wearing the hat.

Another of Bartley's unsuccessful escapades also involved sheep . This time three sheep belonging to a neighbour had gone "missing " . The owner reported the theft to the police. Despite Bartley's reputation for theft , he all but convinced the locals that people other than himself were responsible . He instanced a number of families that were spending an inordinate amount of time drinking in the local pubs He suggested that the stolen sheep were the funding sources for this excessive drinking. His scheming came unstuck when he sold wool to the local merchant . One of the sheep had been a pet lamb at one stage and the owner was able to identify the markings from the wool of this sheep . Bartley was convicted of theft and fined , but this didn't deter him and he continued on his merry way as usual.

Johnnie Quinn, a neighbour of his was suffering constant trespass at his hands. Bartley's sheep hardly ever left Quinn's land. Instead of confronting him, Johnnie invoked the help of another man. This man's sheep had a serious scab disease and Quinn brought the sheep onto his own land. When Bartley saw the diseased sheep, he immediately removed his own and there was no further trespass after that.

These were just a few "setbacks" which don't conform to the general pattern and of course they weren't of the same magnitude as most of his achievements.

THE BEST DEALS

Bartley used to play cards regularly. One evening he was asked by a number of players if he would be playing as usual. Bartley said he wouldn't because he had no money. After some persuasion he admitted to having an imitation coin. He agreed to play with this providing his informants whom he met separately, promised not to tell the others. Bartley won a substantial sum of money using the flawed coin. It was only afterwards when the game was being discussed by the participants that it was discovered that Bartley's false shilling was known to all of them and not just to one as he had led them to understand.

Our hero met a neighbour one day at a fair in Mountbellew . The neighbour wanted to buy a calf .A calf jobber had two young calves to sell and he wanted £18 for the pair but the neighbour only wanted one. One animal was better than the other and was valued at £1 more than the smaller one. Bartley agreed to take the latter but when it came to paying he only paid £8 instead of £8.50. When the neighbour realised the discrep-

ancy he called to Bartley to try to obtain the deficit .
However Bartley pretended to be totally mystified. He said the
calves were £18. Half of eighteen is nine so if one is a pound
less than the other that is only £8. The neighbour failed to convince Bartley of his error and had to live at the loss of his
money.

KEEPING THE BEST TURF TILL LAST

Mary Gavin was another one of Bartley's victims . She owned
a large stretch of bog but because she was elderly she was
unable to harvest the turf Bartley offered a deal to Mary. He and
his family would take turf from Mary's bog and in return they
would provide her with enough fuel. She agreed to this. When
he was drawing the turf, he would have to pass her house. She
was waiting for him on the first day Bartley was ready for her
." Wait until later .1 will deliver yours when we get the good
turf ",he said He used the same excuse which Mary accepted on
a number of occasions subsequently.He finished drawing the
turf without delivering the promised loads and the unfortunate
lady had to make alternative arrangements for her fuel that year.

A FAR SEEING MAN

Another incident concerned a chauffer driven spectacle vendor
who was selling his ware door to door in the area. Having found
out the nature of the business through the grape vine, Bartley

KEEPING THE
HOME FIRES
BURNING !

was prepared for the salesman when he arrived. He welcomed the man and said he was interested in purchasing reading glasses. The vendor was pleased to hear this and was further impressed when his host indicated that he was only interested in the best ones available.However the crunch came when the seller asked "Now Sir, what kind of money would you be prepared to spend on reading glasses (He had expensive ones all of which would have cost more than ten pounds at the time "Well," replied Bartley The last pair I had cost me one and six (approximately seven and a half new pence) and I wouldn't mind spending three shillings on a new pair now". The spectacle vendor left immediately shedding his suavity and manners prior to his exit and declaring that "the miserable bastard should be allowed to go blind."

BARTLEY'S ECONOMY

The " barter" economy was a familiar institution to early business students but the "Bartley" economy was much more relevant to Loughnane's neighbours . An astute observer remarked that Bartley didn't need money. He simply went and got whatever he needed without complicating the issue by the introduction of money.On the other hand he never refused to help anyone. Whatever money he had he was ready to spend and to share his purchases with other people. He visited local houses regularly and was always treated hospitably .As regards work he tried to avoid manual labour as far as possible but liked using horse-drawn hay-cutting machines.When he was in St Bridget's Mental hospital he was asked to barrow stones in a garden. To avoid doing this he kept dumping the stones in the wrong places .As a result the authorities took the barrow away from him and the remainder of his stay there was totally work-free. Legends about Bartley and his deeds are limitless. He had an almost invincible talent for acquiring whatever he needed.

On occasions he had been known to resort to "ghostly" tactics in order to persuade people to acceede to his demands. His skill at lifting things is brilliantly illustrated when he managed to tunnel through a rick of turf. This rick could be seen from the public road and the owner would have been confident that there was no danger of its being stolen. Loughnane had other ideas. He took all the inside fuel for himself and all that remained when he had finished was the shell. The weather was extremely frosty when this occurred and the frost kept the shell of the rick standing. However, when the milder weather came, the rick collapsed and the unfortunate owner discovered that almost all his turf had disappeared.

TAKING TURKEYS FOR A TROT

The turkey market was a big money earner for farmers during Bartley's era. These fowl would be sold in December and the money thus obtained would be used to "buy the Christmas". On one particular year the turkeys in the area began to disappear at an alarming rate. Bartley had "collected" them from various farms and brought them to a secure enclosure. This was Mount Bernard estate with its 15ft. high walls where he held the position of herd for Mr. Rothwell. Eventually someone reported hearing the sound of turkeys coming from the vicinity of the orchard and police came to investigate the matter. On the day they selected, they left their bicycles at Mount Hazel and made their way across fields on foot to the orchard. Bartley's son met Delia Coppinger on his way from Lisheen to Mount Bernard as he was about to feed the turkeys. She told him about the 'strangers" who had left their bicycles close to her house. Bartley's son understood what was happening immediately and when he arrived at his destination he devoted his attention to Rothwell's stock and didn't bother with the turkeys at all. Although he was prosecuted no link was established between him and the stolen turkeys and the case was dismissed for lack of proof. Bartley had a severe temper when roused but instances when he "lost his cool" are rare.

Once he became angry when someone scattered stones from an open air fire and singed his head in the process. Later that evening he arrived at the house of the boy whom he mistaken-ly believed to be the culprit and threatened him with a loaded shotgun. The terrified youth disappeared. However,

Bartley had forgotten the incident by the time the young man returned home and made no further threats against him or his family. Bartley died on January 8, 1960. Perhaps his epitaph can be best sumed up in a statement he once made himself Neighbours were discussing the misconduct of a particular indi-vidual. One of them remarked that it was a pity that the person in question was "on the wrong road". Bartley piped up and said, "Ah no, he was on the right road but he was faced the wrong way". He was a man of tremendous talents and if he had chosen to use them differently he might have been a business tycoon or a famous statesman. As it was he was one of the cleverest men in Galway. if there is a reward for ingenuity in the hereafter then Bartley Loughnane of Ballymacward must surely be one of the wealthiest immortals ever.

CHAPTER TEN
LYDON AT LARGE

RAMBLING AND ROVING

He could be described as a peasant poet, a toe tapping trouba-
dour or a singing spalpeen, but whatever name one selects for
him , there can be no doubting the fact that John Lydon stood
out as a man of talent and individuality among travelling
labourers. Apart from the clothes that he wore, John's sole
worldly possession was a sports bicycle and this remained his
favourite mode of transport during sixty odd years of travelling
throughout Galway. Distance was never an obstacle to him and
he used to cycle from Gurteen to Roscommon and back, a journey or over sixty miles, quite regularly.   In the case of

Fleadhanna, John often managed up to a hundred miles in a matter of a few days. Food, refreshment or a night's shelter rarely bothered him. His main concern was entertainment and the acquisition of medals. However, when John sat down to eat, he always did justice to the meal and rarely left the table until he had disposed of all the eatables.

John Lydon lived with his mother for a number of years in the village of Castleblakeney and worked in the district for local farmers. He was an energetic, hard working man who did quite an amount of manual work, interspersed with periods of unemployment . Whether working or idle, John always managed to set aside for entertainment.

As well as Fleadhanna, John also enjoyed concerts and the country dance houses which were prevalent at the time. His favourite instruments were the Harmonica and the Jew's Harp. He was keen on dancing and one of the highlight's of his career was a dancing stint on RTE'S "Bring Down The Lamp" which was broadcast sometime in the 1970's. Another of John's pastimes was composing ballads and poems. He was a prolific composer and his verses dealt with local, national and international events. Some of his compositions were controversial and couldn't be performed on stage because they failed to pass the local censors. A ballad in this category was one relating to the division of land in Cappalusk. John's best known opus was entitled "The Crowning of the King of Ballinasloe".

DISTURBING THE PEACE

In many ways John was a nuisance. He was a non-stop chatter box who constantly interrupted the conversations of others. In the case of concerts, although few would fault his performances, he generally overstayed his welcome and producers were often reduced to a state of near panic when John failed to respond to their desperate signals to leave the stage. Another thing which annoyed people was his habit of crowing like a rooster as he passed their houses late at mightn't on his way home from dances.

KINDNESS AND GENEROSITY

John was a likeable character who seemed to have a comprehensive knowledge of child psychology. He was particularly popular with children and never failed to amuse them with his antics. In addition to singing, dancing and music, he also entertained them with conundrums and conjuring tricks. Whereas adults didn't regard John as being the "full shilling", children always gathered round to get a closer look at his performances. Material things never really interested John. An All Ireland Fleadh medal meant more to him than all the gold in the world. He was prepared to share the little he had with others and very often produced presents for the children he admired.

POLITICS AND POLEMICS

In political matters John was a radical. He was not regarded as being sufficiently stable to be accepted as a member of any organisation. He was always very forthcoming in his views and politics was no exception. He regarded himself as a republican but he continually annoyed republicans with his professed admiration for the Rev. Ian Paisley. Like many republicans, he regarded a "term on the inside" as a sign of distinction and something of which one could be justly proud. Keeping this in

mind, John set out to achieve his ambition to become a "guest of the nation" in the mid Seventies. He involved himself in a number of arson attacks on the property of local farmers. On the first occasion he set fire to some bales of hay on his way home from a dance in Mountbellew. He was duly arrested and charged with this offence but apart from his own admission of guilt, which no one believed, there was very little evidence to link him with the crime. By finding him not guilty, the authorities had dealt a body blow to his ambition of becoming a prison hero. Another man might have been tempted to give up at this point-but not our John. On a second fire-spree he destroyed more bales of hay and this time his efforts were crowned with success. He was found guilty of arson at Galway Circuit Court and received a twelvemonth jail sentence. He served his sentence in the "Mountjoy Hotel" and enjoyed his stay there immensely. He
became a firm favourite with warders and prisoners alike He often spoke of his intention of returning to Mountjoy to arrange a concert for the inmates, after having been released on completion of his sentence, but he never actually managed to make this "comeback".

For John, his stay in jail meant that he had one up on local republicans, most of whom had never seen the inside of a prison cell. He claimed to have slept in the same bed as Kevin Barry during his enforced vacation. This was undoubtedly the only "all expenses paid" holiday which he ever had. As far as society was concerned, an arsonist had been caught, convicted and imprisoned. However, if one were to asses the situation from John's point of view, it would appear somewhat differently. For him, it meant a year free from tedious manual labour plus free accommodation. It also confirmed his status as "hero-republican" in his own mind, at least.

THE FINAL CURTAIN

Towards the end of his days, Galway Co. Council provided John with a mobile home. He lived in it for about four years. The State gave him a moderate pension and this enabled him to buy food and clothes for himself. He had a gas cooker, radio and television. Occasional agricultural employment ensured that John had a plentiful supply of cigarettes. Life might have continued like this for decades but Fate suddenly intervened. On November First 1979 John failed to make his appearance. Neighbours forced open the caravan door and found John unconscious - apparently the victim of a brain haemorrhage. He died about and hour later before the ambulance arrived having been attended by priest and doctor. Thus ended the career of one of Irelands happiest and most entertaining troubadours. A wet and cold November day saw the coffin of John Lydon being lowered into the grave in Caltra Churchyard. 1979 is often remembered as the year the Pope came to Ireland. For those who knew John Lydon, it will be remembered as the year they paid their final farewell to the Lilting Labourer.

AND JOHN PLAYED ON - AND ON, AND ON.....

THE SECRET OF LYDON'S APPEAL

Though John raised a few hackles in his time, nevertheless he
had a large circle of friends. He was above average intelligence
and had a phenomenal memory. He could recall an in the number of verses and he didn't need a second invitation in order to
recite them. He was familiar with highways and byways in
practically every county in Ireland-having travelled most of
them on foot or by bicycle at some stage.

He had a strong personality and wasn't the least bit shy or hes-
itant. He could be described as a true democrat. In jail he treated prisoner and warder with equal respect while in the outside
world neither cleric, medic nor minister could overawe John
Lydon. Proof of this was evident on one occasion when a
new school was being opened in the locality. Bishops, Ministers
of State and other dignitaries attended and were serenaded by a
large brass and reed band.

Unintimidated by all this pomp and ceremony, John arrived on
the scene, overcoat on shoulder, despite the fact that the weather was very warm, and proceeded to make his way to the main
rostrum. Here he gave the headmistress his name and informed
her that he would be available for school concerts and fundraising events at short notice. The fact that he disrupted proceedings or that he had forced the eminent guests to take a back seat
while he was talking to the headmistress, didn't disturb him in
the least. Although he lived alone towards the end of his life, he
was never lonely or dejected. His mind was constantly occupied
composing new verses or reciting ones which he had already
composed. Unfortunately most of John's compositions have
been lost. Since he died local events have passed unmarked
by verse or poem. Perhaps with the proliferation of videos, discos and electronic entertainment, there is no place for the bard

or poet in our midst any longer. If this is so, then perhaps it is time for us to take another look at ourselves. There is no way in which electronic gadgetry could ever replace toe tapping troubadours of the calibre of the late John Lydon.

CHAPTER ELEVEN

TOM MCDONAGH'S
LIFE OF LEISURE

SNAILING AWAY PEACEFULLY

Tom McDonagh was a low sized man with twinkling eyes and a short moustache. He generally wore a hat. Tom was a droll character not given to over excitement or over exertion. He could be compared to the person who said that he was so fond of work he could sit and watch it all day. For a long time he was employed by the Land Commission in the holdings of the landed gentry which were being redivided among ordinary farmers. Pairs of men were engaged in making ditches of varying lengths and the labourers were paid according to the amount of work that they did. Tom's partner was Patrick Mullins from Ballygreaney. Patrick was a slow but steady worker whereas Tom did little or no work. When the ganger came to inspect the work, he was annoyed at the lack of the pair's progress

"I don't know what to do with the two of you. You're way behind every one else".

"Ah", said Tom, "Wait till me mate wakes up. When he gets into his stride we'll be up with the best of them".

After many rebukes, followed by and ultimatum that they would lose their jobs if they didn't improve, Tom and Patrick had to increase their output. In fact on one occasion they made a dramatic attempt to impress the authorities with their dedication to the job in hand. Tom spotted an engineer in the background and he gave a hint to Patrick that they were being observed. They began to wield their spades at a hectic pace and

the engineer was so impressed that he continued to observe
them for at least two hours. As he was leaving, he remarked to
the ganger that it was a pity that men of this calibre were so
hard to find. The ganger agreed with him but later told a friend
that Tom and Patrick had done more work in those two hours
than they had done in the entire week before that.

After the engineer's departure, Tom and Co. reverted to their
"normal" speed and allowed their blistered hands a lengthy
period of convalescence, while at the same time conserving
their energy for more leisurely pursuits.

GETTING THEIR DAILY SPREAD

At that time, the Land Commission labourers used to congregate for lunch at a local house. Appetites were keen and the but-
tered bread, which was supplied by the people of the house,
used to disappear once the lunch break had begun. Tom decided to do something about the situation. A local woman, named
Maggie Murphy, who had a bad reputation in matters of
hygiene, lived nearby. Maggie and her sister inhabited a shack
with a galvanised roof that didn't have the luxury of a
chimney. Fowl and domestic animals shared the habitation with
the two sisters, and if there was one thing the neighbours dread-
ed more than Maggie's sharp tongue, it was her hospitality. One
day as the labourers were eating their bread and home-made
butter, Tom remarked, "Let them say what they like about
Maggie Murphy but she makes a grand slab of butter"-
(Implying that this was what they were eating.) After this the
men refused the proffered food and Tom had as much butter as
he desired hence forward.

There are many examples of Tom's impishness and buffoonery. Once, a commercial traveller and a butcher were convers-
ing together at a local hostelry. The butcher went to the toilet

"Am I on the right road to Heaven?"

Loughnahinch.

Ruins of Hampstead House.

Alfie Doyle's model of Colemanstown Model Farm.

The old Bog Road at Coolock.

A recent photo of what remains of the gable end wall of Ned Nevin's house.

Ned's transplanted trees.

Another view of Loughnahinch.

and the traveller asked Tom for his name during his absence. When he returned he was very annoyed to be greeted by the appellation "Mr. Scour", the name which Tom had given to the traveller and which the latter used frequently during the exchanges, much to the embarrassment of the butcher, who strangely enough, didn't attempt to correct him. McDonagh's fondness of mischief can also be seen in the following incident. A travelling labourer named Bill King was staying with a neighbour, Tom Manlon. Bill had a reputation for being "light fingered". One night, Tom acquired a Garda cap and called at Manlons saying he wanted to see King. The latter wasn't in at the time but Manlon wanted to know why the policeman was seeking him.

"There have been several thefts in the district and I want to question him about them said 'The Policeman. When King arrived home later, Manlon accused him of being a thief A ferocious row followed and King stormed out of the house declaring he would never again return. Unseen, Tom and his companions witnessed this confrontation from a safe distance. Eventually the irate Manlon returned to bed while the unfortunate labourer had to go in search of accommodation in the early hours of the morning.

WATCH AND PRAY

Tom liked to socialise and was friendly with a local priest named Fr. O'Neill. The two were having a drink one evening when the Angelus rang out. Tom turned from the counter blessed himself and began to recite the prayer. When he finished, his whisky had disappeared, having been disposed of by Fr. O'Neill. Tom didn't accuse his companion of taking the drink but exclaimed,

"There you are now! And didn't 'Our Lord' tell us to pray?"

"Oh no Tom," said Fr. O'Neill, "he told us to watch and pray".

SPARE THE CAN

Tom owned a small farm but continued to "work" for the Land
Commission until fencing ended when the majority of large ~ad
been redivided. When he had retired he used to fetch water
twice a day from a nearby well. A neighbour suggested that he
should use a bucket as this would enable him to bring enough
for the day in one trip. Tom responded "What if I died in the
middle of the day? Then some idling good for nothing 'would
be reaping the benefits of me labour".

One wonders how impressed any legatee would be at the idea
of inheriting a half bucket of unused spring water! Like the
travelling spalpeens, Tom and his fellow labourers have long
since disappeared and there is no trace of the men who converted "Swinging the lead" into a very fine art indeed. Tom's
thatched cottage has also vanished completely and its owner
has found a permanent "resting place" in the parish churchyard.

CHAPTER TWELVE

THE HAPPY WANDERER

In the early part of this century, Ireland seems to have been blessed with a large number of happy-go-lucky workmen. One of these was the late Mick Neary who spent most of his life in Co. Galway. He was a native of Ballymacward, but left the district sometime in the 1920's to seek employment in Britain. While there he visited Scotland, Wales and England and spent some time in the coalmines. He had many exciting stories to tell about life underground. In his work, he met a wide variety of people and was particularly amused by a fanatical religious sect known as the Seekers. These were untiring in their efforts to locate the Saviour. They believed that he could be encountered physically and they used to scrutinise dark corners and move large boulders, hoping to make contact with Him. Mick told them bluntly that whatever chance they had of encountering Lucifer in the mines, the possibility of finding Jesus there was very slim indeed.

While in Britain, Mick was very conscious of his Irish identity and became involved with the Republican Movement in the struggle against the British. Most of his military activities were centred in the Glasgow region and he was given a pension for his efforts by the Irish Government at a later date.

MICK' S MARRIAGE

Mick was regarded as a bit of a Romeo and his name was linked with many members of the opposite sex. However, he didn't sample the joys of matrimony until 1950, when he was almost 60 years of age. His bride came from Crannagh, near Castleblakeney, and was about 10 years younger.

No-one is sure how the two lovers met, and opinion is divided between the local hostelries and the Tuesday market at Mountbellew. The latter venue seems likely, because this was a meeting place for people of all ages.

The wedding which took place in Caltra, is an outstanding event in the annals of local history and is still fondly remembered by all those fortunate enough to be present. Instead of the bride and groom coming to church separately as was the custom, Mick collected his lady-in-waiting (She was waiting by a bush on her own, near Greenville Gates) and proceeded to the church in the company of the entire wedding party in what must have been one very overloaded car.

The wedding was unusual due to the fact that the priest and the bride-to-be, were both hard of hearing. This led to quite a few difficulties during the ceremony and some of these were so hilarious, that a sizeable section of the congregation left the church because they were unable to control their mirth. Towards the end of the Mass the celebrant's temper was reaching breaking point, and this coupled with the tension and the unbridled hilarity of the situation (if you will pardon the pun) threatened to develop into an unpleasant situation. Therefore it was a great relief to all in sundry when Mick and his partner were finally pronounced man and wife.

Mick Neary

THE HONEYMOON

After the nuptials Mick and friends retired to the house of a parishioner where food and drink were provided for the newly-weds and their associates. This was the house where Mick worked as a labourer at the time. Here a tragedy was narrowly averted when one of the guests almost choked while dining as he listened to a retelling of some of the highlights of the wedding ceremony.

After the meal, the bride and groom, best man, matron of honour and some "ordinary guests" again boarded the trusty Ford and set out on the Honeymoon - an entire afternoon at the Galway Races. Although some of the revellers got lost at the races, all were eventually found and returned to base unscathed that evening. The car too, was undamaged apart from the hooter which had worn out as a result of constant blowing. The least fortunate member of the party was the taxi driver. This poor man who had just purchased the car was never paid for the outing. He made several attempts to persuade Mick to honour the debt. However the latter having some slight knowledge of Shakespeare felt that payment "was more honoured in the breach than in the observance" and he never produced the cash. The driver had to console himself with the knowledge that although he received no money, he had played a vital role in one of the most colourful weddings in East Galway.

Economics played a very small part in Micks life. He wasn't noted for thrift. He was much better at entertaining friends in the company of "Uncle Arthur", than he was at earning money for himself and his family. Although the wedding and the honeymoon lasted for just a day, they provided enough material to delight parishioners for decades afterwards.

POST-NUPTIAL ARRANGEMENTS

Mick returned to work the day after the wedding and his wife went home to Crannagh. Here she resided with her contrary brother who refused to admit her newfound husband into the family fold. Micks brother-in-law was convinced that if Mick got his hands on the property, he would sell it at the first opportunity. There were, no doubt, good reasons for this belief, because as mentioned already, our hero's reputation as family provider left much to be desired. Prior to this he had allowed his own house to collapse so I suppose his brother-in-law felt justified in refusing sing to admit him to his abode.

At the beginning there were regular meetings between Mick and his wife. As time went on these became less frequent and eventually they ceased altogether. In later years his recollection of the marriage became so dim, that Mick said he almost joined the unmarried section of pilgrims while attending a retreat in Esker monastery near Athenry. To use a modern phrase, Mick was "financially challenged" but this didn't bother him. He was once asked by a friend how much money he had in his pocket. He replied, "I'm eleven pence ha'penny short of a shilling". As he said himself, his wife would have to live "On half her own wages

HIS FINAL DAYS

Mick and his spouse didn't have any children. Although he didn't have a permanent home, he was always welcome in houses in the locality. When labouring became too much for him, he retired to St. Brendan's Home in Loughrea and it was from here that he made his final journey to Caltra cemetery. (He used to joke that he wanted a private funeral for himself and that he wanted to be buried in Glasnevin which was the largest cemetery in Ireland) It seemed that he fulfilled the prediction of a clairvoyant that he met a half century previously. She foretold that he would die at the age of 94. Considering his life, his work, his heavy drinking, not to mention the hardship being endured while travelling about, his longevity must be ranked as an extraordinary achievement in life of this most extraordinary man.

MICK'S PHILOSOPHY

Mick's attitude can best be summed by the maxim, 'sufficient unto the day is the evil thereof'.

He never worried about the future or the acquisition of wealth. His outlook is clearly in his oft stated opinion that 'Fourpence after your death is lost money'. He enjoyed himself immensely and lost no opportunity of visiting the public house, dance hall or perhaps his favourite place of recreation: the country house ceili.

He had a remarkable memory and such was his powers of recall that he managed to recite a lengthy poem of about fifteen minutes duration shortly before his death. However his best known and most popular recitation was "St. Peter and the Golden Gate". In a poem entitled, "The Dancers the Glen", a local poet wrote:

> "There was always great excitement
> When we had to wait
> For Mick Neary' s lovely version
> Of St. Peter and the Golden Gate.

Mick had a supply of stories and jokes at the tip of his tongue and was ready to display at the proverbial "drop of a hat".

Mick was very skilled also in the field of dialect and often acted as unofficial interpreter to his workmates in Britain. An expression like- "Dye ken yon bar and I'll go for the new-" would leave most of us lost and confused. But not our Mick. He gave an instant translation for another colleague by explaining it thus, "Do you know where the wheelbarrow is and I will get it now He had many funny stories to tell about his life in England. One story concerns a landlord who had been persuaded to attend Mass for the first time. He had been seated quite a while in the church when a regular attender arrived and asked, "Am I late?" The landlord replied "Well I don't know but yon bloke up there has had two drinks already". At that time it was the custom that priests would have their backs turned to the congregation. Occasionally they would face the people in order to impart a blessing. On such an occasion the landlord got up from his seat and was about to leave.

Mick asked him where he was going. "Isn't your man beckoning us out," was the reply.

FOOLING SOME OF THE PEOPLE

As well as stories and recitations Mick liked to play practical jokes on people. At that time crossroad dances and house ceillis were in full swing and Mick's father, Martin, often accommodated gatherings of this kind in his house during the winter. Get together of this kind were not approved of by the clergy and were generally strongly condemned by the priests off the alter. One night when one of these sessions was in progress at Neary's there was a loud knock at the door followed by a short silence. Then the voice of what appeared to be Fr. Pelly, the local PP called out : "Martin Neary what do you mean by getting an old man like me out of bed at this time of night? I'll soon put a stop to this disgraceful carry on". This speech provoked an immediate rush for the door as the revellers exited in all kinds of unceremonious manners. No one noticed that Mick had disappeared shortly before the incident and didn't reappear until it was all over. So effective had been his performance that when he did claim responsibility for the prank, very few of his friends believed him.

Mick also took a delight in scaring late night visitors with ghost stories. He talked of strange ladies that were to be seen in certain places after midnight combing their long dark hair or dogs that appeared mysteriously and continued to follow travellers with open mouths and glaring eyes until they reached their destination, Mick didn't have children but he loved entertaining them. One was always sure of some fun and frolics when his eyes twinkled and when he asked the question, "Where are we now.

Micks family and last journey

Little is known of Mick's mother who apparently died young. His father lived to be relatively old and Mick' s brother was called Paddy. There could hardly be a greater contrast between the two. Paddy was a serious, hardworking individual who was employed as a kind of farm manager and who rarely if ever left his native parish. He predeceased Mick and is buried in the old cemetery in Ballymacward.

Mick asked to be buried in the family plot in Killuane but as things turned out he was buried in Caltra which is also his wife's final resting place. Mick had little time for moaners or begrudgers and enjoyed life to the fill while he was able. He had an erect figure and was active to the end of his life.

If Mick Neary didn't get to Heaven by the grace of God, then one feels he would have used his guile and brainpower to obtain entrance there. One is tempted to ask the question could St. Peter afford to ignore such a likeable character? Anyway if the worst came to the worst and the gates were closed against him, one is confident that he have adopted a ruse similar to the Irishman in St. Peter and the golden gate, who having been refused admission to Paradise, threw his cap inside the gate, thus getting into Heaven at the expense of St. Peter's gullibility.

CHAPTER THIRTEEN

THE OLD BOG ROAD

Imagine the scene. Creaking saws whine as trees are felled and bushes are cut, rocks and boulders make their way noisily on to cart floors. Arms ache and sparks fly as iron strikes stone. It is early morning and small groups of men have just begun to settle down for a day's work, making the old bog road. This project was under the auspices of The Board of Works. In the early 1900's labourers and carters joined forces to remake the existing rut into a structure strong enough to support heavy vehicles. At the time large quantities of turf were making their way from Coolock to all parts of the country, including Dublin, therefore it was essential to have a strong road capable of supporting trucks and lorries. Turntables had to be built to enable these machines to turn without having to drive on to the soft margins.

TO WORK OR NOT TO WORK

Some people worked hard but others were lazy. In order to obtain employment one should be [a] male and [b] married However, one wily bachelor, Eddie Hynes of Keave, when asked about his marital status replied, "Put down engaged", although he was over fifty years old at the time. He got the job even though his status remained unchanged, and he died a bachelor forty years later. Eddie complained to the ganger about the lack of work-breaks. "Damn it", he said, "When I worked in England, I could smoke me pipe and draw me water whenever I liked" He also got into trouble for talking to passersby. For this he was sent to a work-site as far away from the public road as possible. It didn't upset the brave Eddie and he continued to be a thorn in the side of the powers that be during his stint at Coolock.

Of course Eddie wasn't the only one to question the authority of the gangers. Paddy Raftery objected to the idea of having to break stones with a sledge, which he described as 'The last implement of slavery'. Some grievances were genuine Waterlogged drains had to be cleaned and this was difficult for poorly shod workers who didn't have wellingtons. Once a ganger asked an employee to carry bags of cement on his bicycle. Then when a horse died, the workers blamed a local ganger for his death. A group of them gathered outside a house he was visiting and threw some missiles at the door. They called out "Let the horse killer come out now". There wasn't a serious threat to his person but the incident was embarrassing to him. Another unpopular ganger was referred to as 'The man with the lugs'.

A JOB WELL DONE

Disputes or disagreements didn't prevent good solid work from being done Most employees were keen to make progress and worked hard on the scheme. Besides, many of them had a vested interest in the project because either they or their families owned bogs in Coolock. Also the extra money they were earning was a useful addition to their meagre income. In the nighttime roadmaking was a topic for conversation locally. Various plans were proposed, considered and argued over by cottage firesides. Proponents liked to illustrate their theories graphically on the ashes using tongs and pokers.

MATERIALS AND METHODS

Timber and furze bushes were used for 'soling' the road. Sand and cement were required for bridge building , but stones and rocks were the main ingredients Pickaxes and sledges moulded them in shape. The stones were quarried locally from Bolton's quarry in Ballygreaney and horses and carts brought them to where they were needed. Most of the work was done during the winter and although cold and weather caused some problems , nevertheless it suited farmers because it was the quietest time of the year workwise for them.

THEN AND NOW

Gangers employed at Coolock at various times included, Henry Bolton of Ballygreaney, Bill Connaire, Attymon, Tommy Cooke , Keave, Joe Kelly, Kilconnell, and a Walsh man from Connemara. Lorries rarely travel the bog road, nowadays. However, large numbers of tractor-trailers traverse it annually when the local farmers bring home their turf. Repairs to the road have been few and far between. In the forties and fifties there were a few attempts to do so but no work has been carried out on it for several decades. This surely is a tremendous testament~ to those early pioneers who worked there. If the road is to be resurfaced again heavy machines and modern technology will be availed to do the job .Future employees will not have to blister their hands or shed copious quantities of sweat as their predecessors did and never again will the stone-splitting sledges send sparks or splinters showering down on shovel wielding labourers as they do their daily labour on the old bog road.

NED FIGHTS HIS CORNER

Ned Nevin (pronounced Nayvin) was a bachelor who lived where Ballygreaney Coolock and Gurteen-Mountbellew roads intersect. He engaged in land agitation and pioneered stock driving in the district, believing that this would help to speed up land division. He had a small holding and was interested in horticulture. His garden contained a variety of fruits including apples, pears, raspberries and cherries. It didn't have protective walls so Ned had a busy time trying to salvage enough fruit for himself and his friends and to guard it from midnight marauders. He was a keen musician and played a fife in the United Irish League Band. Hunting and fishing were two of his hobbies and such was his pride in the parish that he invited the late Sean Lemass to join him for an angling and hunting expedition.

Ned had and ample supply of fresh water. A tributary of the Corrib flowed by the western side of his house separating him from his neighbour, Jamesie Connor. Then there was a spring well across the road less than twenty yards from his front door. He believed in having the best quality material and possessed a large collection of hooks and a fishing rod and equipment which was the envy of other sportsmen. His fife was first class too and he always handled it with the greatest of care.

PUTTING HIS SHOULDER TO THE WHEEL

Ned was a generous individual whose services were often called upon. His literary skills were excellent and this explained why he was kept so busy with the pen. He could be described as unpaid secretary to the various groups which used his house as a meeting place. He wrote frequently to the Board of Works in connection with the repair of Coolock bog road. He was successful most of the time but he failed at least once. Some tenants wanted the road extended to make a connection with Clonkeenkerrill. Unknown to them at least one opponent was determined that the extension would not go ahead. The extra piece of road would have to go through this man's land and when Ned wrote to the Board of Works, he was told about the objection. Loath to admit failure, he didn't inform the others about the situation.

After a while, supporters of the plan became restless and a delegation was appointed to confront Ned and to rebuke him for his apparent inaction. The principal spokesperson, Joe Ford, was unable to attend the meeting due to illness and the others set out without him. When they arrived at Nevins, Ned had a great welcome for them and in the general discussion and display of hospitality which followed, the main purpose of the meeting was lost sight of and the delegation returned to base without having received a satisfactory explanation as to why the work was not going ahead. Joe Ford, who had got an independent report of the night's proceedings was furious and berated the delegates for their poor performance. He said "First of all ye discussed the entire Bird world (Ned was an experienced ornithologist). If that wasn't enough ye went on to talk about theology and world affairs. To put the tin hat on it, ye filled yer bellies with food and drink and like Judas Iscariot ye passed around the pipe of peace so as o ensure that the whole issue was befogged in a cloud of smoke". (This was a reference to the custom whereby the host lit a pipeful of tobaccco and then passed it around to be sampled by each of the guests in turn. One is a little surprised that Ned would encourage such an unhygienic custom as this.)

In the early part of the century visitors flocked to Ned's dwelling for entertainment and discussion. Sometimes crowds were so large that it was necessary to use two rooms to accommodate the guests. "Separate meetings of the lower and upper house" was how one observer described the situation. Being of sociable disposition and a fluent conversationalist there was nothing Ned liked better than gatherings of this kind.

Ned lived in an era of great political unrest and someone suggested that the place where he and Jamsie resided would be ideal for ambushing the Black and Tans. Ned was taken aback and asked "And what about Jamesie and myself?"

"Well what about ye. Let ye come out and fight for yer country", was the unfeeling answer of the would-be ambusher. Fortunately for Ned and Jamsie the suggestion never caught on and the two men remained undisturbed in their homesteads until their allotted time had elapsed.

Ned's achievements are just a distant memory now and his house and garden are in ruins. Many of the land reforms which he sought have been achieved and the road which he worked so hard to have repaired is functioning well. Mystery surrounds the destination of his sporting gear, his musical instruments and his collection of rods. After his death a selection of his fruit trees and raspberry canes were dumped in the bog where the remained for several years. These were removed and replanted in a domestic garden within the past decade. Strange as it may seem they survived and continue to bear fruit to the present day. Maybe there is a message there for us all. Perhaps some of the good we do may continue after we die.

Energetic people like Ned are scarce. He was a solid unselfish citizen who accepted the trials and challenges of his life and who utilised his talents to benefit others. Our country could do with dedicated and active people of the calibre of the late Ned Nevin.

A King George V medal given to Pat Walsh by the British Army in recognition for his efforts during World War I.

Medals awarded to the Corbett and Stephens families for their services during the War of Independence.

Woodland Station.

Ballymacward Social Centre.

Mannion's thatched cottage.

Sunset at St. Kerrill's Abbey.

The Dolmen at Annagh.

St. Kerrill's Bed.

Crossmaloo.

CHAPTER FOURTEEN

PAT AND LARRY'S FORGE

Walsh's Forge.
This is what is left of the building where Larry and Pat spent so much time shoeing horses.

We conclude our rustic tales with an account of the famous Walsh family of Cappalusk. The last four members to live in Gurteen were Pat, Delia, Katie and Larry. Delia was in America but returned to Ireland for retirement. Katie was in the US also but only spent a short while there. Pat was a World War One veteran who travelled through France and England and Larry spent most of his time working at home.

The Walshs were renowned farriers whose forge was at Cappalusk. The ruins of the forge, which is located almost four hundred feet over sea-level, can still be seen. The last member of the family to work at the business was Larry. He was five foot ten inches high. He had a pale face and was very thin. He enjoyed his work and rated his skill at horse-shooing as being second to none. Most of his customers concurred with this opinion and his services were constantly in demand. This generated a regular income, most of which was used to quench Larry's thirst. All his acquaintances agreed that Larry was a thirsty man. This is not surprising when one considers the nature of the work and the fact that most of it was done in very warm weather. From an early age, therefore, Larry liked to visit the public houses and other places of refreshment. Customers found their patience being tested when they had to wait for his return after a mid-day safari to the local ale houses. However, when he did return all would be forgotten and forgiven as he set to work at the anvil with renewed vigour and determination.

MUSIC TO HIS EARS

Larry loved music and was fond of singing. He won a singing contest organised by a travelling show group and this helped to boost his confidence enormously. Unscrupulous individuals used to take advantage of Larry. They used to praise his skill as a blacksmith or his singing voice and he would reward them with generous supplies of alcohol in return for their compliments. He was innocent in other ways as well. He once told a customer who had a reputation of being mean that he had just met someone who was meaner than he was. Luckily for Larry the local meanie had a sense of humour and was highly amused at the blacksmith's candour.

FORGING CONNECTIONS WITH OTHERS

Unlike the majority of rustics, Larry had a high opinion of travellers (these were the descendants of dispossed peasants, who used to travel around the country in carts and caravans at that time)'The tinkers', as they were called relied heavily on the settled community for their sustenance. He used to welcome them warmly whenever they visited the forge and enjoyed talking to the and about them. He never tired of proclaiming their virtues. Some gossips maintain that he had romantic aspirations relating to certain female travellers but if this was so they never materialised because Larry remained unmarried.

Some of Larry's success can be explained by his familiarity with his customers. He was thoroughly familiar with their requirements. Although modern marketing techniques were not available to him, he knew exactly when horses were due to be shod and when iron rims needed to be replaced on the wheels of the carts. He was slight in build but had a strong constitution and was never known to shirk difficult jobs even in the hottest weather.

As well as being a blacksmith, Larry fulfilled another role in community life. The forge was a meeting place where important issues of the day used to be discussed and where farming operations and business deals could be organised without the necessity of travelling too far. Young men used to help the blacksmith by working the bellows for the fire or by doing other minor chores while at the same time watching the master at close quarters as he moulded chunks of iron into the shape of horseshoes or other farming accessories.

A FAIR CRACK OF THE WHIP

Larry treated his customers fairly and his charges were reasonable. Each patron had to take his place in the queue and was expected to help with the work in hand whenever help was needed. However, Larry was particularly proud of the fact that Bill Smith of Colemanstown, the largest landowner in the district, sent his horses regularly to be shod at Walsh's forge. Strangers were always assured of a warm welcome at Cappalusk. Outsiders who needed his services would be quickly attended and would be sent on their way with a minimum of fuss and at a reasonable charge.

A TERRIBLE TOSS

Larry used to travel on his bicycle to collect the iron which he used as raw material for his work. This was an extremely risky business seeing that Larry was a heavy drinker and that he often carried the iron late at night. He received several tosses while transporting the iron in this manner. One of these was responsible for bringing his career as blacksmith to a premature end. Larry and cargo were upturned one night at the bottom of a steep hill. Although he lived for a number of years afterwards he never really recovered from this accident. Larry retired to St. Brendan's Home in Loughrea and made his last journey from there via the forge to Clonkeenkerrill Cemetery, where the earthly remains of the last Gurteen Blacksmith now lie.

PAT WALSH- A HORSE OF A DIFFERENT COLOUR

Larry was one of the younger members of the Walsh family and Pat his brother, was much older. Pat was a broad shouldered, sturdy man. He was employed as a blacksmith by the British Army and there fore spent a good deal of his time in England. He received a medal in recognition for his work in France during the First World War. The locals reckoned there was no horse in Ireland that Pat wasn't able to control. Instinctively the animals seemed to sense his authority and his presence seemed to produce a calming effect even in the most difficult animals.

Pat Walsh and his sisters, and a neighbour.

Kate, Larry and Delia Walsh.

A BIT OF HORSEPLAY

Pat, like Larry, was fond of drink. He often went on binges which lasted for days. Finding funds for alcohol therefore was nearly always a major problem for him. When he was in England a native of Gurteen heard of his whereabouts and decided to visit him. Prior to the visit, friends advised him not to bring much cash with him and luckily for him he heeded their advice. He found Pat in the company of some weird looking individuals. Instead of conventional clothing they wore shawls and tattered trousers. Much of their attire was held together with nails and pieces of string and they showed scant regard for modesty. They were unshaven and unkempt and it is no exaggeration to say that their outward appearances left much to be desired. When the introductions had been made, the neighbour was ordered to buy drinks for Pat and his companions. The initial rounds were quickly devoured and when the neighbour announced that his money had run out, he was caught, turned upside down and violently shaken. Even the linings of his coat and pants were thoroughly scrutinised before he was released and deposited unceremoniously on the ground. Needless to say, Pat didn't have too many visitors from Gurteen after this incident.

THE BEST OF ELEVEN

When he was sober Pat used to work hard and strange as it may seem had the reputation of being sensible. On the other hand, when had drink taken, his behaviour was sometimes disgraceful. The family was large and Pat being one of the eldest, was expected to set a good example for the others. As can be imagined he didn't always live up to expectations. One evening, after having consumed a large amount of drink, he lay down and began to roll in the gutter outside the local tavern. One passer-by remarked, "isn't it a hard thing for a mother to think that he's the best of eleven.

TAKING THE ROUGH WITH THE SMOOTH

His wild lifestyle seemed to little effect on him because Pat lived to be very old. In later years he looked quite the gentle-man as he drove around in his trap, neatly dressed and wearing a broad hat. Like Larry, he remained a bachelor, but unlike his brother, Pat remained strong and active until the end of his life. Sadly there is no member of the Walsh family remaining. No other parishioner has come forward to carry on the trade of blacksmith, which was so ably performed by Pat and Larry in the days when the plough and the horse reigned supreme and when the name of the Walsh family was known throughout the length and breadth of the county.

Chapter 15
Local Songs and Ballads

The Gurteen Blacksmith

**By John Corbett and
John Mannion**

(I)
Harvest time in Gurteen,
With the Meitheal gathered there
To thrash the stacks of golden wheat,
When all the fields were bare.
Ah those days are full of memories,
Of happiness and of woe,
When Larry shod the horses
In Gurteen long ago.

(II)
Each day he'd blow the bellows,
You could hear his anvil ring.
Twas the sign to all the neighbours
To come and hear him sing.
He'd hammer on his irons,
Mid the forge fires burning glow,
When Larry shod the horses
In Gurteen long ago.

(III)
"Twas then the sweat lines trickled down
The blacksmith's tawney face.
Twas there the athletes hurled
And all the horses raced.
Many dreams were built and broken
In sunlight, rain, or snow,
When Larry shod the horses,
In Gurteen long ago.

(IV)
His eyes would light in wonder
As he hammered on the shoes
And the neighbours came and rattled off
The latest bits of news,
But his mighty strength amazed them
As the talk would ebb and flow
When Larry shod the horses
In Gurteen long ago.

(V)
They would come and they would
linger, While the horses and wheels
were shod. They would help him at the
bellows, Or they'd get some coal or
sods.
Then they gave him payment,
To the Public House he'd go,
When Larry shod the horses
In Gurteen long ago.

(V1)
Through Ballymac and Gurteen,
Through places far and near,
From the highest forge in Con nacht
The sound came ringing clear.
The sound of work and laughter
And conversation low,
Were part of Walsh's busy forge
In Gurteen long ago.

(VII)
That Larry was a mighty smith,
We had great proof of that,
As was his father, Paddy Walsh,
And his famous brother Pat.
He shod the traveller's horses,
As they travelled up and down,
And he shod some great hunters
For James Smyth of Colemanstown.

(VIII)

And when the day's work, it was done,
And sweat upon his brow,
He'd down his sledge and hammer,
And say: "That's all for now."
He'd take the road for James Kyne's pub,
In the tap room he would enjoy,
And when he had a few pints down
He'd sing them 'Danny Boy'.

(IX)

And now the forge is silent,
But the legend it lives on,
Of the mighty deeds the Walshs did
In days that are long gone.
And as we sit and reminisce,
Round our firesides merry glow,
We'll remember that famous blacksmith,
In Gurteen long ago.

STUMBLING STEEDS
KATE O'BRIEN FROM GARAFINE ANDJAMESIE FROM MOYLOUGH

James said "Tis private,"
And Kate closed the door,
Then they sat round the table;
A party of four.
James like a butler all night on his feet,
Told stories of Boston and Washington street.
They're the finest of places you ever could see;
With hundreds of men there ,The image of me.
I'm reduced in me health now and forced to resign,
To come back to Ireland and marry Katie 0' Brien.
Katie was pretty but she wasn't too strong;
The only fault she had of me that me legs were too long.
We had an eight course supper which made our bowels operate;
And down through the garden went Jamesie and Kate.
All round by Clonbrock, then home by Killure,
We drove back by Fohenagh on our wedding tour.
Then the pony got frightened and fell on his pins
And that ended our hopes that we'd ever have twins.
Now I will blame Jamesie and Jamesie '11 blame me;
That we won't have a baby to take on our knee.

James Raftery, a returned yank, married Kate O'Brien from Garafine. These verses refer to an occasion when James visited his loved one at her home. A few neighbours gathered outside to observe the proceedings. Kate took off her apron and hung it on the window in place of a curtain to stop them looking in. However, some of the more inquisitive ones were still able to see what was happening through a hole in the apron. As things turned out the wedding trip ended in disaster too.

STUMBLING STEEDS (2) A HACKNEY' HORSE'S LAMENT

(This refers to an incident in which the owner of a well bred mare sent her to be shod. Unfortunately he didn't have the money for the shoes. The blacksmith refused to let the animal leave the forge until the money was paid.)
From Dublin town to Portadown, I ran the Irish Mail, And Limerick too I swear tis true, Till my legs began to fail.
I won the great Grand National, I slipped at the Galway Plate, And I'm held here now for ransome; With nothing for to ate.
(Those two sets of verses are credited to the Late Joe Kelly of Garafine who later moved to Killaan).

JOYCE'S FALL FROM GRACE

(These lines about the Corgary Landlord who was assassinated may also
have been written by Joe Kelly)

Walter is a noble man,
With steel greys in his Land,
But now he rides a bicycle,
His notions are less grand.

This Walter is a curious lad,
We hear the people say,
He grazes all the land around;
While the tenants starve away.

Now ride your bike if you like
But divide the land you should Sir,
Or we will take it all by force
You'll be minus house and woods Sir.

At the sound the word goes round
Then Walter seems a fool;
Instead of a high bred racer
Sure now he rides a mule.

And when the mule will die
What then will Walter do?
Sell to the Land Commission
And bid it all adieu.

THE GIRL I TIED BEHIND ME

By Josie Hynes

Going down the fall I heard the call
Sever the cord that binds me,
When I looked around,
Flat on the ground
Was the girl I tied behind me.
I tied her on with scarlet cord,
And pulled it oh so lightly
I never thought the cord would break
And leave May Owens behind me.
Go back said Pat and tell Miss Owens,
That here she will not find me,
But I will be standing at Conheeny's gate
With my scarlet cord behind me.
I'm lonely since I crossed the way,
Going down the moorland valley,
Such heavy thoughts my mind doth fill,
Since parting from my Sally.
I'll seek no more the final gaze
For each but does remind me
How swift the cord did give away,
And leave May Owens behind me.
Neary and Roche they did the most,
They treated her most kindly
Her wounds being sore they could do no more
For the girl I left behind me.

THE HAMPSTEAD PUMP

THY WELL BE DUNNE!

T 'was on the 14th of July,
We came to have some fun,
Between the boys of Hampstead
And the honourable Mr. Dunne.
They assembled there that evening
A new pump to erect.
Mr. Dunne said, We'll put it in the centre;
What more can ye expect?
One word borrowed another
Until a row it did arise;
John Maher roared at Richard Bums;
And said he'd blacken his two red eyes.
"You thought t'was no crime," said Richard,
"When you tried to shoot your son."
"My goodness! Ye must be horrid,"
Said the honourable Mr. Dunne.
Paddy Flannery came along the road;
And he talking very loud;
He let a mighty roar off him and frightened half the crowd.
Maggie Murphy made some noise,
And pulled her hand across her snout,
She said "We'll put the pump in Gorrymore and keep the Hampsteads
out."
Lawrence Kenny he came then
His face red as a rose,
He wore a silver watch and chain
And a second hand suit of clothes.
They continued down the avenue
With the shouting and the fun,
They were met by Paddy Varley,
Who shook hands with Mr. Dunne.
Mr. Dunne, he lost his patience,
He said, I'll hear no more.

117

Ye'll get no pump in Hampstead;
Or none in Gorrymore.
I haven't seen a rumpus
Like this, since I've begun.
Your conduct's most appalling,"
Said the honourable Mr. Dunne.
(Mr. Dunne was the engineer responsible for the proposed installation of a
water pump.)

THE FOLLOWING ARE THE ONLY VERSES WRITTEN BY JOHN LYDON WHICH I HAVE BEEN ABLE TO TRACE

THE CROWNING OF THE KING OF BALLINASLOE

by John Lydon
There was a General Election
That was held in Ballinasloe
It was to elect a carnival king
Of the fair and of the Show. The canvassers they went around
They were to elect a mighty giant
That came from Caltra town.
His name is Mattie Giblin,
With his mother all alone He is the heaviest man in Ireland
And his weight is forty stone. They travelled round the country
From Mountbellew to Dunmore,
Around by stoney Dysart,
And home by Ballinamore...
They travelled through Kilkerrin,
Past the blessed well of Scregg,
Around by the village of Clonberne,
And home through the valley of the Black Pig.
Then they went into Glentane Where they did drink their fill
And they had to get long John Roche
To tow them up the hill ....

....

We wish him luck
We wish him health
In 1957
We hope that he'll be king again
And crowned above in Heaven.

THE CASTLEBLAKENEY CARNIVAL

by John Lydon

There was a monster carnival In Castleblakeney town,
T'was run by the local committee Good men of high renown.
They had McDonnell's amusements And the Silver Seven Band,
T'was held in the comer of the town In Captain Kelly's land.
As they marched down Talbot Street,
The banners they looked so grand,
And who did lead the grand parade
But Knockcroghery's Piper's Band.
And now the time is coming,
I think I'll soon retire
For I have blisters on me feet,
From walking round the wire.

THE BANKS OF LOUGLINAHINCH

In the fading glow of twilight When the curlew leaves the bog
Comes the homeward wending farmer
With his horse and car and dog.
And when his work had finished,
He'd come by stream and inch, To fish for perch and eel and pike
From the banks of Loughnahinch.

And on the warm Sundays
T'would often come to pass,
That groups of happy youngsters
Would sit there on the grass. They'd laugh and joke together,
They'd frolic and they'd pinch.
Then they'd walk hand in hand together,
On the banks of Loughnahinch.

They loved to brave its waters. And to make their way across,
To an islet in the centre
With its stones and trees and moss.
And on that wooded islet, Where dwells the swan and finch, One is always
close to nature By the banks of Loughnahinch.

There was music on that islet,
Which reechoed to the shore,
As they danced with one another
On that brightly coloured floor.
It was Father Pat O'Loughlin,
Who provided floor and bench And who organised the boat loads,
Who came to Loughnahinch.

Sixpence was the fee to pay;
Though many thought it dear, For the boattrip and the dancing, Yet they'd
come from far and near. To the first marquee in Ireland, With its trees and
floor and bench, And the
waters danced all round them,
In the shores of Loughnahinch.

A Time and Place For Mirth and Mischief

The crowds kept ever growing
They thought t'would last for years,
But the cruel Irish climate
Soon changed their smiles to tears.
On a fateful Summer's evening
Came a mighty shower to drench
That band of happy dancers
Who had come to Loughnahinch.

Then on a second Sunday outing,
Came another shower of rain,
The dancing on the islet
Was never done again.
No longer did the boatloads come,
By river, lake or inch,
To join in song and music
Round the banks of Loughnahinch.

That place is now deserted,
No fishermen come by;
No farmer on his way from work,
Comes here his luck to try.
And rarely do the revellers
Disturb the lark or finch,
The swans and birds of nature
Live all alone at Loughnahinch.

SOLDIERS, STATESMEN AND SCHOLARS

*Professor Michael Tierney and his wife Evelyn met Pope Pius 12th on a
visit to Rome.*

SOLDIERS, STATESMEN AND SCHOLARS

Hubert and Mary Molloy.
Hubert led the Gurteen Battalion of the I.R.A. in the War of Independence.

SOLDIERS, STATESMEN AND SCHOLARS

Local man Sean Forde gets his degree watched by former Prime Minister Eamonn De Valera – Chancellor of U.C.D.

Prominent republican Michael Cogavin and friends

REPUBLICAN ACTIVISTS IN THE 1916 - 1921 PERIOD

Martin Tierney
(Alloon)

Hubert Molloy
(Attymon)

Tim Scarry.
Second in Command
of the Gurteen
Battalion. Tim lived
in Attyregan later.

Tomas Cormican.
As well as being
entertaining, Tom was
involved in several
anti-British incidents.

SPORTING HEROES – PICTURES FROM THE PAST

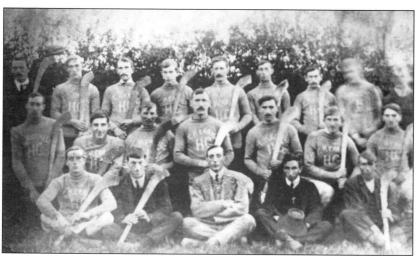

*Galway Senior Hurling Champions 1923. Names include Paddy Bodkin,
Mat Coen, Tom Cogavin, Michael Cogavin, Rick Dilleen, Willie Dillen,
Simon Finn, Larry Griffin, Hubert Molloy, Thomas Molloy, P. Walsh and
Pete Ward.*

*Tom Cogavin who played on the All-Ireland winning team of 1923.
He was the first local man to win an All Ireland medal. He also played in
the post "Bloody Sunday" match in Croke Park.*

PICTURES TAKEN IN THE EARLY PART OF THE CENTURY

Dilleen's Post Office

Gurteen RIC Barracks and Kynes Pub

Burke's Public House and Grocery
as it is today (above) and pictured in 1903 (below).

THE SIGHTS OF BYGONE DAYS

A group of locals relax near Lough na Hinch in former times.

*James Kyne, Dilleen - Murphy and Willie Dilleen (Gurteen P.O.) prepare
for stage in the company of an unknown actor. (He may be Joe Kyne).*

129

	Names of Persons	Place of Abode & Addition	Crime
98.	Martin Coory	Gurteen, Co. G. Labourer	Administering unlawful oaths, conspiring to levy War against the King and adhering to his enemies
99.	John Finn	do.	do.
100.	Mark Newell	Shanbally, Co. G. Blacksmith	A United Irishman and tendering illegal oaths
101.	John Concannon	Menlo, Co. G. Weaver	A Un. Irish. & carry, arms against the King
102.	Owen Huban	Menlo, Co. G. Labourer	A United Ir. for causing the doors of John Jennings to be open by threats & menaces at an unseasonable hour of the night
103.	Hugh Madden	do.	Commanding certain persons to rob Theophilus Blakeney of arms
104.	Michael Connelly	Glanrevagh Co. G. Labourer	Aiding, abetting & assisting in the houghing of cattle
105.	Darby Murphy	Clondrevagh, Co. G. Labourer	do.
106.	Patrick Murphy	Lidanepark, Co. G. Labourer	do.
107.	Michael Higgins	Curradooin, Co. G. Labourer	A United Ir. and administering unlawful oaths
108.	John Kinamore	Lidanepark, Co. G. Labourer	Aiding and assisting in the houghing of cattle
109.	Andrew Farrell	Gorrymore Co. G. Labourer	Being one of an armed party who assembled on the lands of Lisloughlin to assist the French
110.	Patrick Hart	Gurteen, Co. G. Labourer	do.
111.	John Finn	Colemanstown Co. G. Miller	Being one of an armed party who assembled on the lands of Lisloughlin to assist the French
112.	Patrick Connelly	Gurteen Co. G. Weaver	do.
113.	Patrick Connor	Kilturas, Co. G. Labourer	do.
114.	Patrick Cogavin	Gorrymore, Co. G. Labourer	do.
115.	Francis Kirwan	Rock Lodge, Co. G. Esqr Lieutenant in the L.A. Yeomanry	Tendering Illegal Oaths, exciting persons to hough and maim cattle, extorting money and comparing to murder the Reverend Mr. Wood and the Revd Mr. Mangen
116.	Richard Summerill	Cussane, Co. G. Labourer	Houghing and maiming cattle.
117.	Patrick Kenny	Roundfield, Co. G. Labourer	do.
118.	Patk McHugh	Toneraw, Co. G. Labourer	Tendering unlawful oaths and exciting persons to hough and maim cattle
119.	Daniel Haneen	Shanbally Co. G. Labourer	Houghing & Maiming cattle
120.	Bryan Naughton	Biggery, Co. G. Labourer	Taking and carrying away the flesh of houghed sheep & exciting persons to hough & maim cattle

	Names of Persons	Place of Abode & Addition	Crime
50.	Richard Semmerill	Cussane, Co. G. Labourer	Administering or assisting to administer Unlawful oaths
51.	Patrick Lally	Cockstown, Co. G. Labourer	Assisting in administering unlawful oaths
52.	Gill Henson	Faravane, Co. G. Yeoman	do.
53.	James Gavin	Kurkamo Co. G. Labourer	Delivering threatening letters thereby to extort illegal contributions
54.	John Houghegan	Ballyglass C. G. Herdsman	Forceably carrying away the flesh of houghed cattle
45.	John Jones	Hampstead Co. G. Schoolmaster	Houghing & Writing & Sending threatening letters to different gentlemen thereby to raise illegal contributions
56.	Thomas Losby	Cooloo, Co. G. Labourer	Houghing & Maiming Cattle
57.	Bryan Fahey	do.	do.
58.	Michael Higgins	Moat Co. G. Labourer	do.
59.	John Conway	Kilkeran, Co. G. Labourer	do.
60.	James Leneghan	Coolo, Co. G. Labourer	do.
61.	Patrick Coleman	Granna, Co. G. Carpenter	A United Irishman
62.	Patrick Murphy	Oughlageen Co. G. Labourer	Tendering & obliging persons to take unlawful oaths
63.	Michael McWalter	Oughlageen Co. G. Labourer	do.
64.	Edmund Staunton	do.	do.
65.	John Staunton	do.	do.
66.	Miles McWalter	do.	do.
67.	James Donohue	do.	do.
68.	Mathias Doherty	Oughlaggen Co. G. Labourer	Tendering and obliging persons to take Unlawful oaths
69.	Michael Thornton	Maughranore Co. G. Yeoman	Houghing & Maiming Cattle
70.	Patrick Griffin	Oughterard Co. G. Yeoman	do.
71.	John Griffin	do.	do.
72.	Francis Brennan	Galway in Co. of town of Gal. Flaxdresser	A United Irishman and endeavouring to administer unlawful oaths.
73.	John Hardiman	Ahascra Co. G. Shopkeeper	A United Irishman & appearing in arms as a rebel
74.	James Hardiman	Ahascra Co. G. Carpenter	do.
75.	Michael Kearns	Tuam Co. G. Flaxdresser	Houghing, Robbery and tendering illegal oaths
76.	Patrick Naughton	Castle Kelly Co. Ros. Labourer	do.

	Names of Persons	Place of Abode & Addition	Crime
121.	Thomas Finn	Killoclougher, Co. G. Labourer	Tendering unlawful oaths
122.	John Cahill	Glynvamin, Co. Clare Labourer	do.
123.	Edmond Cosgrave	Barratna, Co. G. Shoemaker	Wilful & corrupt perjury before the martial court
424.	William Noon	Menlo, Co. G. Labourer	Administering unlawful oaths, appearing in arms as a Rebel & for houghing and maiming cattle
125.	Patrick Ryan	Ahascra, Co. G. Labourer	Being one of an armed party who assembled on the lands of Lisloughlin to assist the French
126.	John Gillane	Listonavarone, Co. Clare Labourer	Accused of Treasonable and seditious practices
147.	Pat Tierney	Gurteen Co. G. Weaver	do.
128.	Jeremiah Mahony	A private of the Co. Limerick Regt of Militia	do.
129.	Thomas Power	do.	do.
130.	Bartholemew Finn	Private of the Co. of Sligo Regt. of Militia	do.

14.   PROCLAMATION

Whereas Information had been received, that certain Persons, charged with Treasonable Practises, are still at large in parts of the County of Galway, and places bordering thereon : His Excellency the Lord Lieutenant, desiring to restore the same good Order to the District aforesaid, which happily exists in other parts of this Kingdom, does hereby require all Persons therein, who have been engaged in the late Rebellion, and are, by the Act of Amnesty, or any former Proclamation, entitled to pardon, upon certain Conditions, to proceed without delay, for the purpose of receiving Certificates and Protections, to the Officer Commanding nearest to which they reside.

And his Excellency the Lord Lieutenant does hereby order, for one month from the Date thereof, that there shall not, in the District aforesaid, any arrest or molestation of any person whatsoever so entitled to Pardon, take place, for any Act done in furtherance of the Rebellion.

And whereas certain other Persons, charged with having committed Crimes not entitled to Pardon, continue to lurk and conceal themselves in the District aforesaid.

His Excellency the Lord Lieutenant does hereby appoint a like time of One Month from the date hereof, for all such persons (save as hereafter named), to repair to any Garrison Town within the said District, there to surrender themselves to the Officer Commanding and give sufficient Security to depart forthwith (in a vessel to be provided for them) from the Dominions of his Majesty, and not to return into the same without Permission.

And his Excellency does hereby order, that all Persons not excluded from the Pardon aforesaid (save as hereafter named), in whatever degree they may have offended shall be allowed to pass without molestation, to the said garrison Towns, within said District, for the purposes aforesaid, for the space of One Month from date thereof.

A document, courtesy of Galway Archaeological and Historical Society, detailing local involvement in the 1798 rebellion.

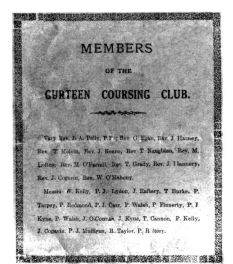

Gurteen Racing Card

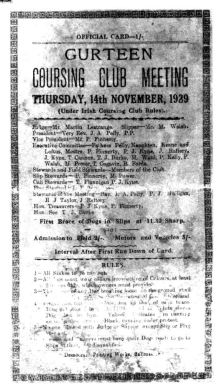

SOME LEAVES FROM HISTORY PAGES

FUNERAL OF MR. O'CONNELL.

From the earliest dawn on Tuesday, the 3d inst., the gates of Marlborough Street Church were besieged by crowds of anxious individuals of both sexes, and on the opening of the church at six o'clock, it was at once filled in both aisles and galleries. The sacrifice of the mass then commenced to be offered at the high altar, and the two smaller ones also. As each clergyman concluded he was succeeded by another, and thus the mass was offered up continuously during canonical hours for the soul's eternal rest of the departed. The means for entrance into and exit from the church were at different ends of the building, and thus as one congregation departed, another succeeded from the vast crowd outside. In preparation for this solemn and melancholy occasion it is supposed that not less than twelve or fourteen hundred dignitaries and clergymen of the Catholic Church have already arrived in Dublin.

The solemn obsequies for Mr. O'Connell took place on Wednesday, the 4th. For more than two hours before the time appointed for the commencement of the obsequies, every approach to the church was crowded. The admission was by tickets, issued by the Cemeteries Committee ; and though many were disappointed, all the church could contain were accommodated.

The interior of the church was clothed in mourning, and in every way fitted for the occasion. The muffled windows scarcely let in the light of day, but four hundred wax lights in chandeliers cast a sombre effulgence on the dark scene, which added much to the imposing effect of its solemnity and its grandeur. Directly in front of the altar was the catafalque, on which the coffin containing the remains of O'Connell rested ; it was covered with black cloth. A canopy, supported by four pillars, was raised over the upper dais or platform, on which the coffin was placed. From each of those pillars projected a chandelier of exquisite workmanship. The four chandeliers cast the brilliancy of twelve lights on the lid of the coffin. Lower down were twenty-four lights, and lower down again thirty-six around the catafalque. The front gallery was set apart for the immediate friends and relatives of the deceased. In it were the four sons of Mr. O'Connell—Maurice, John, Morgan, and Daniel—with many other relatives, and several of the ladies of the family. In front of it was the O'Connell arms, with the supporters, motto, and crest in the form of a hatchment. On the sides and ends of the upper dais of the catafalque the arms of the family were emblazoned. Over the front door we saw them also on stained glass, on a white ground, diapered with shamrocks, and surrounded with a border of the same national emblem. In the corners of this stained glass was the Irish harp, and the initials D.O.C. in ornamental letters of golden hue. In front of the organ loft, and around the catafalque were suspended scrolls, on which were written in Latin the inscriptions adopted at the obsequies at Rome.

Before eleven o'clock the church was filled. The aisles and galleries were occupied by the laity. The nave was reserved for the clergy. The ladies present commonly wore some emblem of mourning. The office commenced a little after eleven. The nine lessons of the nocturns were read by nine of the prelates present. The grand high mass commenced as soon as the office had terminated. The Venerable Metropolitan, the most Rev. Dr. Murray, presided.

The funeral oration was preached by the Rev. Dr. Miley. He described O'Connell's victory in death, his fame at Rome and all over the world. He gave an eloquent account of the obsequies in Rome—of the journey homewards—of the passage through the Alps, their reception in France and in England — asked where could O'Connell be rivalled among the great men of the past—vindicated O'Connell's principles in language forcible and eloquent, alluded to O'Connell's sincere devotion to his religion, and to the new link by which he has bound Ireland to Rome by sending his heart there, dwelt feelingly on O'Connell's great love for the Irish people, and expressed his conviction, that the suffering of the poor in Ireland had pressed so heavy upon him as to hasten his death, and concluded by recommending that O'Connell's remains be interred near his childhood's home.

The solemn absolution which the Pontifical prescribes in offices, for a pope, a bishop, or a prince, was given over the remains of O'Connell. This interesting ceremony, so seldom celebrated, and which gave to O'Connell the dignity of a prince in the Catholic Church of his native land, was thus performed ; — The five senior bishops, the Most Rev. Drs. Murray, MacHale, and Nicholson, and Right Reverend Drs. Keating and Whelan, left the sacristy in black copes, followed the master of the ceremonies to the catafalque, and took their positions at the respective corners, the celebrant remaining at the head. Each in turn then gave the usual absolution prescribed in the Roman Pontifical. And thus ended the most solemn obsequies ever celebrated in Dublin.

Whether we regard the number of persons, the solemn order with which the ceremony was conducted, the air of religious zeal which pervaded the moving masses, and the melancholy occasion upon which they had assembled, we must pronounce the procession of O'Connell's funeral the most imposing spectacle ever beheld in Ireland.

THE FUNERAL SERVICE OF DANIEL O'CONNELL IN THE MARLBOROUGH STREET CHURCH, DUBLIN.

604   16 November 1490   *Reg. Lat.* 894, fos 87^r—89^r

To Cornelius Oconcemynd, canon of Tuam, mandate. The recent petition of Malachy Ymanyn, cleric, d. Tuam, stated that while in the church of Clonfert there is a distinction of prebends and each canon of that church lives separately[1] the canons of the same hold in common the tithes of Cloncayncaryll, Cilmoind, Kilmoluy, Gortanmullayd, Killechan Nagarne alias Killaedhamair, Kilcunach and Kilmardlanacosne, places in the diocese of Clonfert, lawfully belonging to their capitular *mensa*, but that through the carelessness of the said canons, the dean of that church has taken the said tithes, without any title or support of law in respect of them, but temerariously and *de facto*, for a certain time, as he still does unlawfully and unjustly. At Malachy's supplication for the erection and institution of a canonry and prebend in that church, for his life, and for the assignment to them of the said tithes—of which at present the canons take nothing—as dowry, the pope hereby orders the above canon to summon the bishop of Clonfert, the chapter and dean of the said church and others concerned, to erect and institute a canonry and prebend in the said church, for Malachy's life, without prejudice to anyone, to constitute and assign to them the said tithes as dowry, and to collate and assign the said canonry and prebend, of which the annual value shall

not exceed 3 marks sterling, thus vacant as being newly erected, to Malachy, if he is found suitable upon examination, inducting him etc. and causing him to be received as a canon, having removed the said dean and any other unlawful detainer.[2] Notwithstanding any statute fixing the number of canons in that church, etc. The pope's will is that on Malachy's death or resignation thereof, the canonry and prebend shall be extinguished and the said tithes shall return *eo ipso* to the capitular *mensa*.

Piis fidelium votis gratum nos decet prestare assensum . . .
S. de Castello | P | P x Non Kal' Januar', anno septimo [24 December 1490], *Altissen*

1. *seorsum et per se* (fo. 87^r)
2. sc. from possession of the tithes

THE ROYAL VISIT TO KILKEE.

(Air : SHAN VAN VOGHT.)

(At a specially couvened meeting of the
Kilkee Town Commissioners, attended by
Mrs Griffin, Messrs Bry n Sheedy, John
Quinlian, Batt Hennessy, John Purtill,
Joseph Corry, Michael Taylor, Michael
O'Shaughnessy, and Michael Corry, an
invitation was extended to the King and
Queen to include Kilkee amongst the
places to be honoured by a Royal Visit.
A loyal address was also unanimously
adopted on the motion of Mr B Hennessy,
seconded by Mr J Quinlan; and Mrs AMY
GRIFFIN and Mrs BRYAN SHEEDY
were deputed to present it.)

Oh ! the King is on the sea,
　　Says the Shan Van Vocht,
And he's coming to Kilkee,
　　Says the Shan Van Vocht ;
And what a precious pair
To greet him will be there,
On behalf of poor West Clare,
　　Says the Shan Van Vocht.

Oh ! 'tis they can tell a tale,
　　Says the Shan Van Vocht,
Of poor old Granuaile,
　　Says the Shan Van Vocht,
And her sons, compelled to roam
Far across the ocean's foam,
Or to live as slaves at home,
　　Says the Shan Van Vocht.

When the spokesman of the town,
　　Says the Shan Van Vocht,
At the royal feet kneels down,
　　Says the Shan Van Vocht,
Will he shook the royal ears,
By telling of past years,
And the people's woes and tears ?
　　Says the Shan Van Vocht.

Of the plundered and oppressed,
　　Says the Shan Van Vocht,
In the desolated West,
　　Says the Shan Van Vocht,
And the banished and the dead,
From Kilmurry to Loop Head—
Will he tell you *that*, King Ned ?
　　Says the Shan Van Vocht.

Of the rack rent and the writ,
　　Says the Shan Van Vocht,
And the fatal Notice to Quit,
　　Says the Shan Van Vocht,
And the crowbar in the wall,
And the roof tree's crashing fall—
Will he tell you that at all ?
　　Says the Shan Van Vocht.

And beside the bailiff there,
　　Says the Shan Van Vocht,
See, there kneels a lady fair,
　　Says the Shan Van Vocht,
Whom the crawling Papists, bent
To the earth like dastards, sent
Their poor town to represent,
　　Says the Shan Van Vocht.

Will she tell the King and Queen,
　　Says the Shan Van Vocht,
Of the days of Henry Keane,
　　Says the Shan Van Vocht,
Who upon our sainted sod,
Where the feet of Senan trod,
Tried to bribe us from our God ?
　　Says the Shan Van Vocht.

Will she keep them in the dark,
　　Says the Shan Van Vocht,
About Father Meehan's Ark,
　　Says the Shan Van Vocht,
And the Saviour forced to roam
Without Temple, House or Home,
Save the blue of heaven's dome ?
　　Says the Shan Van Vocht.

Oh ye crawlers of Kilkee,
　　Says the Shan Van Vocht,
May your names detested be!
　　Says the Shan Van Vocht.
You've besmirched your Country's
　　fame,
You've disgraced your Church's
　　name—
May your lot be endless shame !
　　Says the Shan Van Vocht.

PICTURE SHOWS.

STRONG CONDEMNATION BY THE BISHOP.

(TO THE EDITOR.)

Ashline, Ennis

Dear Sir—I hope the people of Ennis
will note well the revelations made by Mr
P. J. Linnane at the last meeting of the
Urban Council, about the pictures shown
at the Town Hall. Every man in Ennis
should be grateful to that worthy gentle-
man for drawing public attention to this
scandal.

We now know how foul the stuff on
which our young people are being fed in
that hell-shop.

Our duty is clear and unmistakeable.
It is to shun the place as infected with a
plague.

It is said it brings £200 to the rates. It
takes double that amount out of the town,
and from the very class who can least
afford it. But are we for any price, however great, sunk to the level of those vile
wretches who live on white slavery.

It is suggested to have the films censored
by a local Committee. It is hopeless. I
doubt if there are decent films enough to
last a week. These films are not made in
Ireland for the Irish mind. They are made
in England and America for a people
steeped in sensuality. We may check them
for a week or two But Satan will bide
his time, gradually thickening the dose
until our palate will relish the worst he
can serve.

No, the sooner this source of corruption
leaves our little town, the better for Ennis
It should never have come there. The
Town Hall is no place for it; I ask the
people to shun its doors. No girl especially
should enter them. Let us shun its doors
and they will soon close.

I am, yours sincerely,

✠ M. FOGARTY,
Bishop of Killaloe.

SINN FEIN NOTES.

(As passed by Censor.)

The chance Ireland pines for has
come at last. Within a month the
voice of the nation will be heard declaring for Independence without re-
serve and without limitations. This is
the first election in the history of Ireland in which the issue—Ireland a nation or Ireland a British Province—is
to be put clearly before the people,
and the people will answer as they
have answered always. In the words
of a brave man who died in our gene-
ration "The instinct of the people
has always been unerring."

* * * *

The time in which we have to prepare for the task is short; Sinn Fein
is a young movement which has had a
marvellously rapid growth. We have
not that vast machinery which belongs
to the older political organisations, but
we have youth and strength and enthusiasm. It is for us to translate
that youth and enthusiasm into language—into the voice of a nation demanding through the Poll, the right of
the Irish people to freedom.

A contemptuous English Minister
has said we are not fit for freedom. We
are less worthy than the Czecho-Slavs
—nay, we are not fit for that miserable measure of Home Rule which
denies us the collection of our own
taxes. How will Ireland answer that
contemptuous sneer? It is by returning men who will cross the Irish Sea to
whine for favours from the proud, superior English? We are a nation
older than England and our faith in
Ireland a Nation is stronger than the
British Empire.

* * * *

We have but a few days to accom-
plish work that lies to hand, and to do
that work satisfactorily Sinn Fein
needs the assistance of every man,
woman and child who believes in the
future of our race. It is not sufficient
now to think right; it is necessary to
act right—and the way for each to act
is to place his or her help at the disposal of the Election Committee in the
various districts.

* * * *

These Committees are new to the
work in practically all the constituencies and the help of everyone is needed, because the election takes place
everywhere on the one day, and every
constituency will be thrown on its own
resources to a great extent. Therefore
everyone who sees the all-importance
of having a voice
termination being clearly heard should
be at the disposal of

134

Miscellanea.

Monument at Clonkeen, Co. Galway.—Mr. Wakeman forwards a rubbing, and a reduced drawing of an inscription, both of which refer to a much neglected monumental effigy of a bishop, now lying in the cemetery of Clonkeen, near Tiaquin, Co. Galway. He writes :—

"In Brady's 'Episcopal Succession,' vol. ii., the following notice occurs :—'1718, Edmond Kelly succeeded "per mortem ultimi illius

Epiœopi." His Brief was dated in February, 1718. He wrote to Propaganda on the 14th of May, 1718, to announce his consecration, which had been performed in Dublin, with three bishops assisting. His faculties as bishop were granted on the 15th November, 1718. In April, 1733, Clonfert was vacant.'"

Proposed Destruction of Kilmallock Castle.—At a meeting of the Council of the Royal Society of Antiquaries, it was proposed by Mr. George Coffey, M.R.I.A., seconded by J. J. Digges La Touche, LL.D., and passed unanimously :—"That the Council of the Royal Society of Antiquaries of Ireland has heard with regret that a Presentment has been passed by the Presentment Sessions for the Liberties of Kilmallock for the purpose of taking down the King's Castle at Kilmallock.

"The Council is surprised at the contemplated act of vandalism, inasmuch as the preservation and protection of ancient and historic monuments is recognised as a matter of great public interest, and trust that now

THESE ARE PHOTOCOPIES OF LETTERS WRITTEN BY PADRAIG PEARSE TO LOCAL MAN SEAN MACGIOLLARNATH (SEAN FORD)

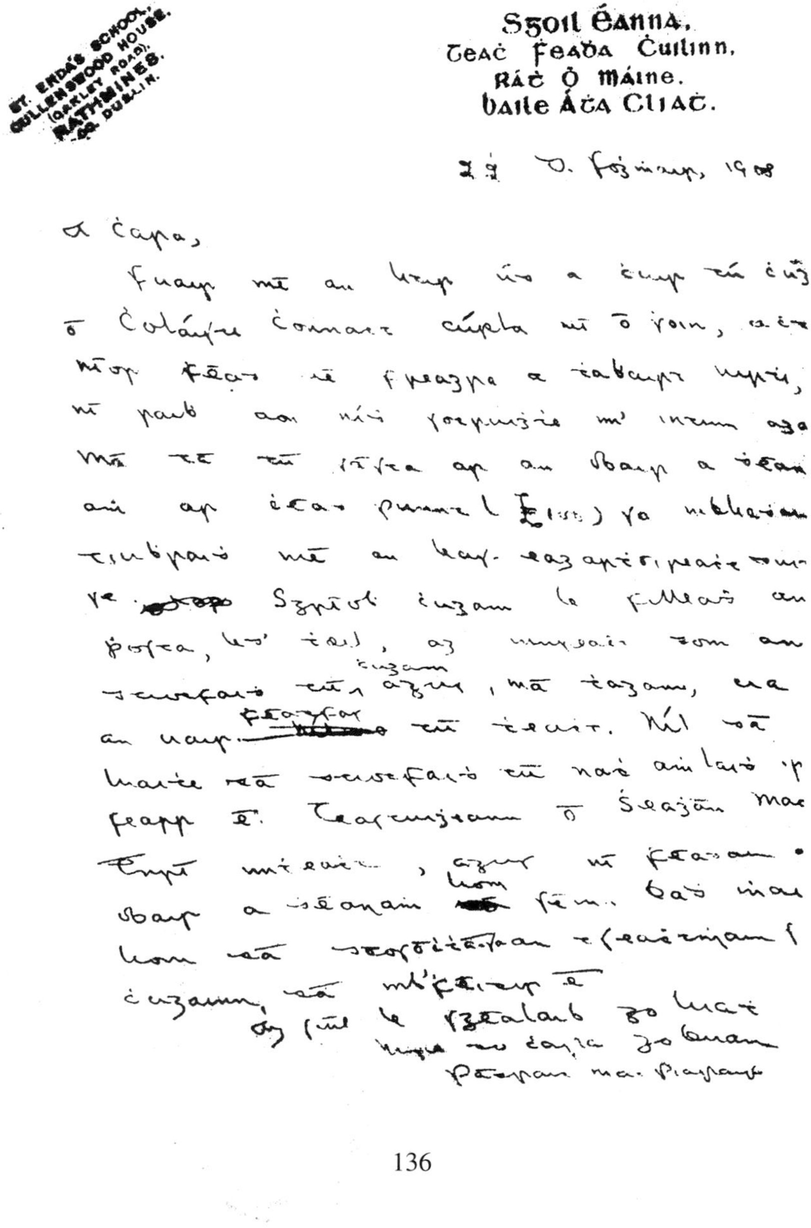

Sgoil Éanna,
Teaċ Feaḋa Ċuilinn,
Ráṫ Ó Máine,
baile Áṫa Cliaṫ.

23 O. Fóġmar, 1908

A Ċara,

[handwritten letter in Irish, largely illegible]

Sgoil Éanna
(ST. ENDA'S COLLEGE).
Ráth Fearnáin
(Rathfarnham).

30 Aib. 1913.

A chara,

[handwritten letter in Irish, largely illegible]

beir buaidh 7 beannacht.

pádraic mac piarais.

137

Glossary

An Claideamh Solais=Literally The Sword of Light- a revolutionary publication edited by Padraigh Pearse.

An Cruiscin Lan=The full jug- a plentiful supply of alcohol.

Back sliding=Reneging on promises.

Biddy Early=a wise woman who lived in Feakle, Co. Clare more than a century ago. She was noted for her extraordinary healing powers.

Big Noise=Important person.

Black Cow=Porter or beer.

Board of Works=A semi-state organisation responsible for the upkeep of by-roads etc.

Brideogs =Ceremonial images of St. Bridget.Groups of people sometimes combine to play pranks on others at the time of the celebration of the Saint's feastday.

Bring Down The Lamp=A programme of traditional music which used to be broadcast on R.T.E. television.

Buachaill= boy

Cailin(colleen)=girl.

Camogie=a ladies' hurling game.

Caper= odd or unusual behaviour.

Clogs=heavy wooden boots which used to be worn by farmers.

Contraption=machine or instrument.

Constable= police officer(A member of the R.I.C.)

Cunnies=workers or natives of Connemara.

DEV.= Eamon De Valera, a revolutionary leader who founded the Fianna Fail party.He was Taoiseach (prime minister) on a number of occasions and served two terms as president of The Irish Republic.

To drag ones feet =to idle.

Dresser= cupboard or place for delph.

Elbow grease=exertion or energy.

Eleven pence ha'penny short of a shilling=almost out of money.

Fairs=Farmers used to bring farm animals to be sold on the streets and side walks of local towns.These have been replaced by marts.

Farrier= one who takes care of horses.

(Not)the full shilling=mentally unstable.

General absolution=absolution given to penitents without the necessity of repeating their sins to a confessor.

God spare you the health =verbal thanks.

Guest of the nation= a prisoner.

A horse of a different colour=completely different.

I.R.A.=Irish Republican Army.

Letter to me=wrote to me.

Light-fingered= inclined to steal things.

Macra na Feirme =literally Sons of the farm:a society dedicated to the promotion of rural values. It organises debates, public speaking and a variety of talent competitions.

Mo chara= my friend.

Mountjoy Hotel=Mounjoy Prison in Dublin.

On the wrong road=behaving badly.

Pioneer= one who abstains from alcohol.

Playing to the gallery=trying to impress onlookers.

Pump=(a) a water system/
(b) to inflate a bicycle tyre.

Putting the cart before the horse=not doing things properly.

Putting ones shoulder to the wheel--making a proper effort.

Quarry (a) a sand or stone pit.
(b) someone who is being pursued.

Rambling houses--houses where neighbours used to gather regularly for recreation.

R.I.C.--The Royal Irish Constabulary.(This was the force employed by the British government to police Ireland prior to 192 1.)

Scor na n-oG=a talent contest for young people sponsored by The Gaelic Athletic Association.

Sez= says.

Soling the road =preparing the road for surfacing by giving it a solid foundation.

Spalpini,spalpeens= travelling labourers (mostly from Connemara.)

Taoiseach-- literally chief. In-practice the prime minister of the Irish Republic.

Term on the inside=a period of imprisonment.

Top dress= farmyard fertiliser.

Tops of the Clubs==a talent competition for various clubs.

Toppin' man =Well done.

Treading the light fantastic= dancing.

Turning the tables=getting revenge on someone,or a completely different situation.

Uncle Arthur= alcohol.

Yon=That over There

Yowl=Literary the devil -an expression of anger or surprise.

Appendix-Introduction

Ballymacward Social Centre is a spacious building once used extensively for dancing, discos and concerts. One of the great dancing sessions was on Christmas night and this attracted massive crowds from all over the country. The centre was constructed using money from the prize bond win. Seamus Duffy~ and his committee invested a large amount of money which they had collected from plays and concerts in the bonds and were lucky enough to win first prize (approximately £5,000). This allied to other fundraising ventures helped to pay for the project in a short time. Seamus and his family lived at Esker where he taught for many years. After that he took up a teaching post in his native Mayo. He is very interested in traditional music and singing and is actively involved with Comhaltas Ceoltoiri Eireann. The centre is used for meetings nowadays. Many parishioners have devoted free time to the supervision of functions there over the years none more so than the present caretaker, Johnnie Kenny of Hampstead.

Gurteen Parochial Hall was originally a church which was converted to a hall. As in Ballymacward, people in this side of the parish have made tremendous contributions to its development. It was reroofed and remodelled a number of times and was the venue for countless concerts and dances. St. Kerrill's night always topped the league for attendance's and another outstanding event took place in 1954 when stars from Radio Eireann, as it was then called, featured there.

In the showband era nearly all the big bands played in one or other of the parish halls. They were both used for basketball, badminton and other indoor sports at various stages.

John S. Flynn has written a scholarly and well presented book on the history of the parish. This is an invaluable work which should be read by all those who are interested in past events in this area. John and his family live in Dublin and have a deep affection for the locality. John's daughter, Mary, is a fine singer who has performed on R.T.E. television.

John Scarry was a scholar who from an early age had to make his own way. He travelled by train to Galway to pursue his studies and deserves great credit for his efforts to educate himself on a limited financial budget. He worked with Irish Press Ltd. and suffered a stroke in his fifties. He died relatively young.

Martin Finnerty was once a member of Galway Co. Council. He was a tall, active man who wrote several articles about the history the area. He was particularly interested in early history and the saga of St. Kerrill. Some of his writings are still available thanks to his namesake, Martin Finnerty of Clonkeenkerrill.

Sean MacGiollarnath or Sean Ford was a distinguished scholar and law man and the enclosed are copies of letters which pass between himself and Padraig Pearse. Sean Ford of Galway, his grandson, kindly made these available. It is said that Sean MacGiollarnath knew the location of every poitin still in Connemara. When asked why he didn't take action to deal with these he replied that his job was to deal with the cases that came before him and that he would leave the task of hunting law-breakers to the police. He is related to the Coppinger family of Killuane.

Professor Michael Tierney was prominent in politics in the early days of the state. He is related to the Tierney and Ward families of Alloon.

Tommie Roche has been a leading light in local life for decades. He is a clever, successful and likeable character and his inventions have helped to improve the quality of life throughout the country. Although he worked for a short time in England, most of his life was spent in the parish where he still lives with his family.

Tom Kenny was related to the Brodericks. He was a tall, broad-shouldered man, whose strength was unknown. He worked at Ford's shop which at that time was a thriving business concern.

CHAPTER ONE- APPENDIX

Much has been written about Fr. Griffin who is related to the Dooley and Lyng families. Those wishing to know more about him should consult Fr. Lee's biography which was published some years ago.

Fr. Pelly was a formidable man. He possessed a valuable art collection and had an active interest in sporting affairs, especially coursing. He had a thorough knowledge of post-famine land tenure. Many regarded him as a "bigshot" who favoured the upper classes. One parishioner called to him for a reference for his son who wanted to go to college. Fr. Pelly didn't give the reference and suggested that instead of going to college ,the youth should find work in a local public house. The parishioner's wife was scandalised when she found that her son's reference came from the Protestant minister at her husband's behest.

Fr. Naughton was a devil-may-care, always ready to enjoy himself, yet sometimes, he was easily angered. Rumour has it that he put a curse on Larry Murray of Killuane who refused to supply him with fuel one bad winter. Larry said that he would supply the fuel the following year and Fr. Naughton is supposed to have said "You will, if you are still there". The curious part of the incident was that Larry and his wife Essie both died within the year.

Fr. Michael O'Reilly was a determined man who didn't brook opposition. During World War 2 he actively encouraged the removal of swastikas and other emblems which young pro German supporters had erected on poles. He claimed that the swastika was a reversion of the Christian cross. He spent many years in Duniry after leaving Gurteen and died in his eighties.

CHAPTER TWO - APPENDIX

Fr O'Loughlin was a popular ladies' man. The evidence shows that he was a pastor with boundless energy and determination

CHAPTER THREE - APPENDIX

Cormican was a jovial figure, always ready for devilment. He had one daughter who married John Kelly and they and their family live in the village of Corsgeagh. Tom was active in Republican circles and was involved in the incidents referred to in the introduction.

CHAPTER FOUR - APPENDIX

Corbett's house was purchased from Larry Murray's relatives when it was auctioned in 1929 The purchaser was James Stephens from Cranny in Co Clare who was working at Woodlawn station at the time. He later purchased a farm near his native village and Murrays holding was transferred to his sister and her husband.

CHAPTER FIVE - APPENDIX

Dennis Flynn's grandchildren and his daughter-in-law inhabit the house where Dennis and his late son Paddy once lived. Kathleen Costelloe, his daughter, live next door and his other son John, and his family, reside in Dublin.

CHAPTER SIX - APPENDIX

Jimmy Joyce spent a long time in the parish. His grasp of the English language didn't improve with the passage of time. He rarely mentioned home or relatives and was content to spend his life working and drinking in the parish. Rows of Connemara workmen used assemble around the square in Athenry. On Sundays in Spring, Summer or Autumn farmers would engage them for a week or fortnight. After partaking of refreshments they and the hired men would travel to the farmers house (usually by horse and cart) Work was less plentiful in winter and wages were lower than at other times of the year

CHAPTER SEVEN - APPENDIX

Pat was a no nonsense man who liked to get things done. His son John lives on the family farm and Nora, his daughter is married to Jimmy Kelly and they also live at Cappalusk. Pat was related to the Walshs whose exploits are also dealt with in this book.

CHAPTER EIGHT - APPENDIX

Stories and legends about St. Kerril abound. St. Dubhan's name has been recorded in the book of saints but attempts to get information on Kerrill have proved fruitless .This hasn't lessened the veneration for him and the belief that he descended from royal Irish stock is still strongly held especially in Gurteen . There is a photograph of the chapel at Inverness which was founded in his memory at the rear of St. Michael's church.

CHAPTER NINE - APPENDIX

Nearly every parishioner has a selection of Bartley Loughnane stories. All of them serve to confirm his reputation as a person of ingenuity and resourcefulness. His family married locally but never involved themselves in the kind of deeds which made Bartley's name a byword in east Galway.

CHAPTER TEN APPENDIX

John's life centered on stage appearances and entertainment. He had a phenomenal memory and could recite passages from songs and poems effortlessly. Nearly all of his compositions have been lost,and the ones which are reproduced here were unearthed by John Mannion of Cappulusk. Lydon loved to give the impression of being "with it". In Summer, he used to dress in shorts and t-shirts and his attempts at sun-bathing were often frowned upon by the more conservative members of the community. He had blue eyes and golden hair which maintained its distinctive hue up to the time of his untimely death. He was an avid reader and even his failing sight didn't deter him from pursuing this hobby.

CHAPTER ELEVEN - APPENDIX

Tom was a droll character who spent most of his free time at Kyne's public house His cottage in Gorrymore was burned shortly after his death - His work for the Land Commission helped to provide him with whatever pocket-money he needed.

CHAPTER TWELVE- APPENDIX

Neary stayed at different houses at different times. He was employed by the Stackpoole family but reports indicate that he never allowed work to distract him from his main purpose in life -entertainment.

CHAPTER THIRTEEN - APPENDIX

Ned had no direct heir. His property is now owned by Sean Ryan of Attymon.

CHAPTER FOURTEEN- APPENDIX

The Walshe's had a long tradition in the horse-shoeing industry They were justly proud of their reputation which attracted many outsiders to their forge. Their sister Katie acted as house-keeper for them in later days and saw that her brothers always fulfilled their religious duties. Once, when Larry had retired, a friend advised him to stay at home from Mass because of frosty roads Katie was furious when she heard about this and confronted the friend saying,"When did you become Larry's spiritual adviser ?".The poor blacksmith was obliged to set off for church despite the inclement weather.

CHAPTER FIFTEEN - APPENDIX

The Gurteen Blacksmith first appeared in a magazine published by St. Kerrill's Festival Committee in 1993.

Walter Joyce is mentioned a few times in this anthology. It was to his house that Bartley Loughnane fled when he became "insane". Land agitation led to Joyce's death. He was shot on his way tao Mass and his killers were never caught. The parody on The Girl I left Behind Me was one of several ballads composed by Josie Hynes.

The author of Hampstead Pump is unknown. However, it has been suggested that a deceased member of the Kenny family from that Village was responsible. The Banks of Loughnahinch was written to remind people of the many happy Sundays which our ancestors spent there.